LUKE

A Devotional Commentary

LUKE

A Devotional Commentary

Meditations on the Gospel According to St. Luke

GENERAL EDITOR

Leo Zanchettin

the WORD among us

The Word Among Us
9639 Doctor Perry Road
Ijamsville, Maryland 21754
www.wau.org
ISBN: 0-932085-27-X

Third Printing 2000

Cover:
St. Luke by Edward Mitchell Bannister
National Museum of American Art, Washington DC/Art Resource, NY
Cover design by David Crosson

Made and printed in the United States of America.

Foreword

Dear Friends in Christ:

Of the four gospel writers, no one gives us so many richly developed character portraits as St. Luke does. Whether he is telling us about the prodigal son running into his father's arms, Zacchaeus climbing the sycamore tree, or the repentant woman anointing Jesus' feet, Luke shows us people whose lives are radically changed by an encounter with the love of God the Father and the healing touch of Jesus. This, in fact, is one of the central messages Luke sought to proclaim: Everyone who comes to the Lord can be changed.

Luke is careful, however, not to make this sound automatic. Yes, each of us is invited to come to the Father through Jesus, but we can only come through the door of humility. Throughout his gospel, Luke shows us that it is the quiet, the repentant, and the prayerful whose lives are changed. They are the ones who understand that without Jesus they have no hope or purpose to their lives.

What was true for Luke's audience in the first century of the church is just as true for us on the brink of a new millennium. Jesus is our only hope. He alone can heal our wounds, forgive our sins, and reconcile us to the Father. In this devotional commentary, we have sought to emphasize these truths to help you experience Jesus in a personal and life-changing way. Our prayer is that, whether you pick up this commentary only on occasion, or whether you use it every day as you read through the entire Gospel of Luke, you will come in touch with Jesus and your heart will be changed. May we all run to him with the simplicity of Mary Magdalene, John the Baptist, and countless others who have gone before us.

We want to thank everyone who has made this commentary possible. Many of the meditations produced here were initially developed for *The Word Among Us* monthly publication, and we want to thank all of the writers of these meditations for granting us permission to reprint their work. In addition, we want to thank Fr. Joseph Mindling, O.F.M. Cap., and Gregory Roa for their contributions. And in a special way, we thank Patricia Mitchell, without whose contributions and editorial skills this book would not have been possible. May the Lord abundantly bless each of them.

Finally, in this year dedicated to God our heavenly Father, we want to ask the Holy Spirit to reveal to all of us the mercy and compassion of our God. Day after day, he calls us to himself. May we all respond with open, humble hearts.

Leo Zanchettin
General Editor

Table of Contents

An Introduction to the Gospel According to St. Luke

By Fr. Joseph A. Mindling, O.F.M. Cap.

Our curiosity about the authors of the New Testament always seems to outrun the sparse information that survived the church's early years of dispersion and persecution. Nevertheless, we do have this brief description of the man behind the Third Gospel in an anonymous manuscript dating back to about 160 A.D.

Luke, a Syrian of Antioch, a physician by trade, was a student of the Apostles. Later on he was a disciple of Paul until the latter's death. Having served the Lord faultlessly, having remained unmarried and without children, he passed away, full of the Holy Spirit, in Boethia [in northeastern Greece] at the age of 84. As gospels had already been written by Matthew in Judea and by Mark in Italy, Luke, under the impulse of the same Holy Spirit, wrote his gospel in the region of Achaia [in central Greece]. In his prologue, while acknowledging that other gospels had been written before his, he explained that it was necessary to present to the faithful converted from paganism an exact account of the economy of salvation, lest they should be impeded by fables or caused to stray from the truth by the deceit of heretics.

The prologue to which this text refers, Luke 1:1-4, introduces us to Luke's "orderly account" of what took place in Jesus' earthly life. Then, Luke goes on to refer to the "things which have been fulfilled among us," moving us to think about the way Jesus' words and actions set a pattern that had a profound influence on his followers "from the beginning." By producing a two-part composition, Luke was able to demonstrate how the earliest successes and sufferings that he described the church experiencing in the Acts of the Apostles echoed those of the Master that he narrated in his gospel. In effect, this beloved physician prescribes a regimen for spiritual health and growth: Seek to know Jesus as his first followers did by making his story a part of your life.

The central and most powerful message of Luke is that *Jesus willingly embraced death on the cross for us and that the Father affirmed this act of love by raising him from the dead*. This proclamation is in complete harmony with the witness of the rest of Apostolic Church, but each of the writings in the New Testament presents the good news in a distinctive way, and Luke's Gospel is especially rich in unique contributions. Before settling in to work through its treasures one passage at a time, let us identify some of these features which give a special perspective to Luke's portrait of Jesus.

A Portrait Drawn with Words

An ancient tradition claimed that St. Luke was not only a talented history writer but also a skillful artist. Although we have no first-century canvases that can verify this legend, Luke's ability to engage the human imagination is quite literally "on display" in the countless books and museums that contain depictions which are, in fact, graphic illustrations of his gospel. How many painters have sought to show Gabriel greeting the Mother of the Messiah, or to capture angelic choirs singing "Glory to God in the highest" to the wide-eyed wonder of shepherds and sheep? Only Luke records these moments, and several others of similar renown: the pint-sized public official, Zacchaeus, up in a sycamore tree (Luke 19:1-10); the consoling words of Jesus to a criminal who accepts his own crucifixion (23:39-43); and an evening walk to Emmaus with the engaging Stranger who was concealed in the flesh but who revealed himself in the breaking of bread (24:13-35).

Some of the most memorable scenes in this book are sketched by Jesus himself in his parables: the gardener giving the fig tree one more year to make good (Luke 13:6-9), the contrite tax agent outpraying the self-satisfied Pharisee (18:9-14); and the father with arms wide open to welcome a long-sought son—one who had hit bottom but who was saved by coming home (15:11-32). The message in all these parables is not new to those acquainted with the other gospels, but each of these pictures in Luke highlights the conviction that Jesus sought to proclaim about his Father: He is ready to show compassion long before the offender can even figure out an apology.

A Gospel to Pray With

Using these and other images to lead our imaginations into more meaningful contact with Jesus is already an important part of what a book of meditations is about. The purpose of a devotional commentary is to help us to lift our minds and hearts to God, and to respond as we discover him seeking us in the scriptures. This goal was obviously one of the important motives underlying the composition of Luke's gospel because he returns so frequently to this aspect of Jesus' life. Not only does he record Jesus' instructions about praying, he shows us how Jesus himself maintained a rhythm of prayer that accompanied all his decisions and activities. It is also to Luke that we are indebted for the texts preserved in the canticles of Zachary, Simeon and the Blessed Virgin Mary (Luke 1:68-79; 2:29-32; 1:46-55). Those who recite the Liturgy of the Hours continue to make them part of the church's living voice of praise and thanksgiving every day.

When we turn to a section of the scripture like the Gospel of Luke, we know by faith that this is God's word. Through it he communicates with us as individuals, just as he uses it to speak to us as members of a family, or a parish, or as members of the human race. But faith needs to sharpen our expectation that the Lord has something to share with us that is related to the specific circumstances of our life, the "right here, right now" of our personal history. And with the help of the same scripture, we find the words to speak back to God.

We can make good use of this gospel as a prayer aid by coming to it as active listeners. We can ask what prompted Luke to include the special features that attract our attention. We can be creative in seeking parallels between our own personal journey and the events of Jesus' life. Most of the time believers approach these stories by reading relatively small excerpts and examining them in discussion, through a homily, or in personal meditation. This is quite fitting, because even brief passages contain abundant food for reflection. It is also important, however, to watch for the way several shorter sections link together to outline aspects of Jesus' attitudes or his way of acting that are too extensive to be portrayed fully in any one episode.

Jesus' Universal Concern

One of the frequently revisited themes in Luke is the striking openness of Jesus toward every group of people that needed his attention and the power of his love to restore people. Luke has a fresh way of underscoring this sensitivity of Jesus with small but significant details, or sometimes by bringing in whole new episodes or incidents. It is especially evident in the way Jesus shows concern for the marginalized members of society, like the poor, widows and orphans, those stricken with leprosy, or victims of prejudice, like the Samaritans.

In a similar vein, Luke reports several instances in which Jesus interacted with women in meaningful ways. For modern readers this may not seem surprising, but for first-century Palestinians such initiatives could be a jarring experience. All the evangelists report that Mary Magdalene and her female companions were chosen to be the very first people to announce Jesus' resurrection, acting as apostles to the apostles. But Luke's narrative goes further than any of the others in the actual number of women it mentions and the information it gives about some of the important ways they figured in our Lord's ministry. It even gives us the specific names of a few women we would not otherwise have: Elizabeth, Anna, Joanna, Susanna, and Mary, the mother of James (Luke 8:1-3; 24:1-11). Although modern readers may know nothing more about these people, we all instinctively understand the significance of being recognized and appreciated as an individual, and of being remembered by name.

Luke's careful accounting ranges from the precious material he saves about the Virgin Mary, to the women who accompanied Jesus on his preaching tours, to the unnamed and unconventional admirer who anointed the Master's feet and dried them with her hair (Luke 7:36-50). And where else would one expect to find a parable in which the character representing God is a winsome peasant who throws a big party over the recovery of a single coin—something perhaps insignificant to others but very precious in her own eyes (15:8-10)?

Jesus' Special Interest in the Poor

A second area where the alert reader can profit by noting Luke's technique of "revisiting themes" concerns the value of detachment from material possessions. Matthew, Mark, and John all depict Jesus as unencumbered with physical possessions, instructing his disciples to conduct their missions in a similarly austere way, and demonstrating a constant concern for the poor. But Luke sharpens this message by including several teachings of Jesus not recorded elsewhere:

In the parable of Lazarus and the rich man, Jesus cautions that there are dire consequences in the afterlife for those habitually insensitive to the poor who are on their doorstep (Luke 16:19-23). In the parable of the rich man, who thinks only of hoarding wealth for himself, Jesus reminds us of the passing nature of worldly goods and the precariousness of earthly life (12:16-21). Finally, attending a banquet held by a prominent religious leader, Jesus tells his host to invite the poor and the handicapped to his celebrations, precisely because they cannot afford to invite him back (14:12-14). Again and again, Luke reminds his readers that almsgiving and renunciation of personal possessions are the ordinary prerequisites for those who want to follow Jesus.

Open to the Spirit of the Gospel

As we listen and pray our way through this gospel, we can appreciate the richness of the text more deeply if we continue to look for passages where Luke shows Jesus, not only as a noble figure who incites awe, but as a model who inspires imitation. Is this too daunting a challenge? Where do we find the ability to understand and the courage to adopt the ideals Luke has preserved in these pages? Not surprisingly, he has anticipated this question and has woven into the gospel one further major element, a theological thread which binds others together in a meaningful way. This, of course, is Luke's quiet but persistent interest in the role of the Holy Spirit.

As in the Old Testament, the Holy Spirit is the power of God, responsible for the conception of Jesus and his anointing at baptism. The Spirit guides him into the desert and empowers his mission and miracles. Luke tells us that, after Jesus' ascension, the same Spirit descended upon the disciples. He bestowed on them the understanding, talents and confidence they needed to follow Jesus. He taught them to conform their hearts and minds to Jesus and to share their vision of him with a new generation

As we journey on now into the Gospel of Luke and the reflections that accompany it, we pray that the Spirit who long ago inspired Luke to write so engagingly will also help us to hear accurately and to receive enthusiastically whatever awaits us in these pages.

The Enlightened Imagination

Meditating on the Life of Jesus with St. Francis de Sales

By Patricia Mitchell

If we want to use scripture to enrich our prayer life, there are many spiritual advisers to whom we can turn, but St. Francis de Sales is one of the masters. In his spiritual classic, *Introduction to the Devout Life*, de Sales recommended that prayer center on the life and passion of Jesus because he is the supreme model for how Christians are to act and think.

Francis de Sales was born in Savoy, France, in 1567, and was consecrated Bishop of Geneva in 1602. In addition to co-founding the Institute of the Visitation order with St. Jeanne Frances de Chantal, he provided spiritual direction to many people, often through long letters. *Introduction to the Devout Life* came out of these letters and reflects the pastoral wisdom, love, and gentleness for which de Sales became famous. He died in 1622, at the age of 55.

The method outlined by de Sales is especially useful in praying through a gospel like Luke's, because Luke is filled with richly detailed scenes that can move us deeply. We can imagine the prodigal son, returning to the warm embrace of his father. We can see the good Samaritan picking up the wounded man on the road. We can envision the baby Jesus lying in a manger, with the host of angels singing his praises. We can talk with the risen Christ on the road to Emmaus. Each story or event is filled with treasures to unearth.

In his writings, de Sales provided detailed instructions on how to prepare to meditate on an event or story in scripture and how to apply the lessons we have learned to our own lives. In a very simple but effective way, he outlines how our imagination, our intellect, and our emotions can work together to bring us closer to the Lord.

Using the Imagination

De Sales outlined his method in Part II of *Introduction to the Devout Life*, which is dedicated to the necessity of prayer. The first step is to place ourselves in the presence of God. We do this by stating in faith that God is present in all things and all places, especially in the very center of our hearts. Using our imagination, we can picture Jesus gazing down on us from heaven, or we can envision him "as if he were near to us, just as we sometimes imagine a friend to be present."

The next step is to ask God for his grace. In this "invocation," we can use words from scripture, such as: "O God, cast me not away from your presence and your Holy Spirit take not from me" (Psalm 51:11), or "Let your face shine upon your servant" (Psalm 31:16).

Having quieted our hearts and asked the Lord to be with us, we are ready to meditate on a specific passage from scripture. Imagine choosing Luke 23:32-38, perhaps, where Jesus forgives his persecutors from the cross. According to de Sales, we should use our imaginations to construct the entire scene in our minds. "Imagine that you are on Mount Calvary and that there you see and hear all that was done or said on the day of his passion."

Using the imagination in this way has an underlying benefit—in keeping our minds engaged so fully, we are less likely to become distracted. As de Sales wrote, Our minds "will not wander above, just as we cage a bird or put a leash on a hawk so he can rest on our hand." De Sales placed such a strong emphasis on the imagination because the goal of these "meditations," as he envisioned it, is not to study the scriptures in a scholarly way or to learn more on an intellectual level. Instead, the goal should be to "acquire virtue or love of God."

Going Deeper—The Intellect

After we have fully imagined the scene, we now use our intellects to consider what we have read in the passage and what we have envisioned in our minds. We should do this calmly and unhurriedly. If one image or one phrase especially strikes us, we should remain with it, asking God to teach us more. If not, we should simply move on to the next point.

Perhaps we are struck by the picture of Jesus—bruised and beaten—walking to his death, accompanied by two criminals. We might envision the expressions on his fellow prisoners' faces—the "good thief" beginning to repent for his sins, and the other one hardened in a look of fear and defiance. Then we might think of Jesus walking—in pain, but peaceful, knowing he was in his Father's hands. "How do I react to suffering?" may be the question that comes into our minds. "How did Jesus act, and how can I take on more of his attitude?" "Imitate the bees," de Sales wrote, "who do not leave a flower as long as they can extract any honey out of it."

Affections and Resolutions

In the process of imagining Jesus on the way to his cross, we might find ourselves feeling a sense of sorrow over what he suffered, or loving Jesus more for what he has done for us. We may feel moved to become more like him in forgiving those who hurt and malign us. These feelings, or "affections," are the product of our meditations, and we can readily recognize in them the work of the Holy Spirit opening our hearts. However, de Sales recognized that there was one more step to take. He called on his readers to transform these feelings into "special and particular resolutions" that we can make for our own "correction and improvement."

For instance, if we want to become more forgiving, then we can make a "resolution" not to be hurt by those who treat us poorly or speak offensively to us. Instead, we should think of ways we can please them. In this way, as de Sales observed, "you will correct your faults in a short time, whereas by affections alone it would be a slow, difficult task."

Conclusion and Spiritual Bouquet

Finally, we bring our meditation to a conclusion with prayers of thanksgiving, especially for the ways God has stirred our hearts—the "affections"—and for the decisions to change our lives—the "resolutions"—he has led us to make. In this prayer of thanksgiving, we offer our lives to the Lord and ask our Father to give us his grace and to bless our resolutions so that we can faithfully fulfill them. We also intercede for others, asking that the same grace that we have received would be poured out upon the church, our pastors, and our friends and relatives.

In order not to lose the fruit that has been gained from the meditation, de Sales recommended gathering "a little devotional bouquet":

> People who have been walking about in a beautiful garden do not like to leave without gathering in their hand four or five flowers to smell and keep for the rest of the day. In the same way, when our soul has carefully considered by meditation a certain mystery we should select one, two, or

> three points that we liked best and that are most adapted to our improvement, thinking frequently about them, and smell them spiritually during the rest of the day.

The grace we have received from our meditation can stay with us if we "gently transfer" our hearts from prayer to other duties, while striving to preserve the feelings our meditation has aroused. Throughout the day, we should act on the resolutions we have made, always looking for any occasion, however big or small, to do so.

Francis de Sales was convinced that we can come closer to Jesus—and become more like him—by observing his words and actions. He compared this process to little children learning to speak by listening to their parents and "lisping words with them." It is in the gospels that we can find Jesus—praying, healing, teaching, and loving us to the point of death. Through the grace God gives us, our time spent meditating on the gospels will transform us, and help us to become like our beloved Savior.

The Story of Christmas

LUKE
1–2

Luke 1:1-4

[1] In asmuch as many have undertaken to compile a narrative
of the things which have been accomplished among us, [2] just as
they were delivered to us by those who from the beginning were
eyewitnesses and ministers of the word, [3] it seemed good to me
also, having followed all things closely for some time past, to
write an orderly account for you, most excellent Theophilus,
[4] that you may know the truth concerning the things of which
you have been informed.

Luke wrote his account of the life of Jesus so that Christians might "know the truth concerning the things about which [we] have been informed" (Luke 1:4). To know the truth is to know Jesus as the Messiah, the Son of God, and through believing, to have life in his name. God wants to give us life in abundance. He does not want us to live in bondage to fears, anxieties, bitterness, or hatred.

Jesus has come to set us free, to release us from our captivity and give us a brand new life of faith through the power of the Holy Spirit. That is why he could declare: "The Spirit of the Lord is upon me. He has sent me to proclaim release to the captives and recovering of sight to the blind, to set at liberty those who are oppressed to proclaim the acceptable year of the Lord" (Luke 4:18-19). Spiritually and physically, Christ can set us free.

Christ gives us the opportunity today to say "yes" to him; to stand in faith and declare him as our salvation. Often we go to the Lord with our problems but are unwilling to give up ways of thinking or acting which are keeping us in bondage to these concerns. If we believe that Christ is our salvation, then we ought to "feed" on the word of God often during the day. We should kneel in prayer from time to time and open our minds to the revelation of the Spirit, taking God's commandments and the example of Jesus as the rule for our lives. This is how we come to know the truth—the truth that sets us free.

Troubles may come our way; sorrow or illness may afflict us. Yet Jesus was sent to bring the good news, to set us free from all that oppresses us. Faith is all that is required on our part. Let the truth of Christ be our deliverance. And what is that truth? That God sent his only Son, Jesus, into the world to die for our sin. On the cross his blood was shed and the ransom paid so that we could be released from enslavement to sin and be reconciled with our Father as his sons and daughters—co-heirs with Christ. Let us pray: "Your words, Lord, are spirit and life. We want to live in that new life today and every day."

Luke 1:5-17

5 In the days of Herod, king of Judea, there was a priest named
Zechariah, of the division of Abijah; and he had a wife of the
daughters of Aaron, and her name was Elizabeth. 6 And they
were both righteous before God, walking in all the
commandments and ordinances of the Lord blameless. 7 But they
had no child, because Elizabeth was barren, and both were
advanced in years.
8 Now while he was serving as priest before God when his
division was on duty, 9 according to the custom of the
priesthood, it fell to him by lot to enter the temple of the Lord
and burn incense. 10 And the whole multitude of the people were
praying outside at the hour of incense. 11 And there appeared to
him an angel of the Lord standing on the right side of the altar
of incense. 12 And Zechariah was troubled when he saw him, and

fear fell upon him. [13] But the angel said to him, "Do not be
afraid, Zechariah, for your prayer is heard, and your wife
Elizabeth will bear you a son, and you shall call his name John. [14]
And you will have joy and gladness, and many will rejoice at his
birth; [15] for he will be great before the Lord, and he shall drink
no wine nor strong drink, and he will be filled with the Holy
Spirit, even from his mother's womb. [16] And he will turn many
of the sons of Israel to the Lord their God, [17] and he will go
before him in the spirit and power of Elijah, to turn the hearts of
the fathers to the children, and the disobedient to the wisdom of
the just, to make ready for the Lord a people prepared."

Why did God choose Zechariah and Elizabeth as people through whom he would work out his plan of salvation? Surely there were some in Israel who were younger, stronger, or more learned. Yet he chose to employ an elderly priest and his barren wife. He saw something of great value in these upright and obedient Jews (see Luke 1:6). They were among the remnant of Israel which had remained blameless and faithful to the law of the covenant.

Through the cooperation of such as these, the Father would begin the long-awaited fulfillment of his promise, working through the son born to them. As parents use discipline to train their children and prepare them for adulthood, so Yahweh (through the law) prepared his faithful remnant to receive grace through Christ.

Zechariah and Elizabeth raised their son John to revere and obey Yahweh. God set John apart from his infancy to be the herald of the good news. Having entrusted him to godly parents, the Father also filled him with the Holy Spirit (see Luke 1:15). The psalmist anticipated what John would live: "My mouth will tell of your righteous acts, of your deeds of salvation all the day, for their number is past my knowledge. O God, from my youth you have taught me, and I still proclaim your wondrous deeds" (Psalm 71:15,17).

John the Baptist lived these words and cooperated with God's plan. Because John allowed God to form and use him, he was able to announce clearly the coming of the Messiah, and prepare the people to receive their Savior. It is easy to pass over John the Baptist as we center on Christ, but we need to see what God planned to accomplish through John and how John cooperated with God so it would be fulfilled. While the work of Christ would bring his people to the fullness of grace, the law prepared them by teaching them the way of God and bringing them to the threshold of grace.

We can prepare for a deeper coming of Christ into our own lives by taking up God's plan in practical ways. Are we taking responsibility before God for the truth that has been revealed to us? If we are parents, are we loving and caring for our children (even adult children) by teaching them the ways of God? Such questions can help us to focus on God's plan. As we do, we will be more disposed to receive God's teachings with open hearts.

Luke 1:18-25

18 And Zechariah said to the angel, "How shall I know this? For I
am an old man, and my wife is advanced in years." 19 And the
angel answered him, "I am Gabriel, who stands in the presence
of God; and I was sent to speak to you, and to bring you this
good news. 20 And behold, you will be silent and unable to speak
until the day that these things come to pass, because you did not
believe my words, which will be fulfilled in their time." 21 And
the people were waiting for Zechariah, and they wondered at his
delay in the temple. 22 And when he came out, he could not
speak to them, and they perceived that he had seen a vision in

the temple; and he made signs to them and remained dumb. [23]
And when his time of service was ended, he went to his home.
[24] After these days his wife Elizabeth conceived, and for five
months she hid herself, saying, [25] "Thus the Lord has done to me
in the days when he looked on me, to take away my reproach
among men."

Zechariah experienced a life-changing encounter with the angel Gabriel. It is easy to assume that God was "punishing" Zechariah for his lack of faith. In reality, God's love for Zechariah was so immense that he sought to ensure that Zechariah grew in humility and peace. Jesus came to bring us many things, but the virtues of peace and humility are among the gifts that he most delights in giving his people.

As he began Zechariah's story, Luke made sure to tell us that Zechariah was a good and upright man (see Luke 1:6). Would any of us have fared any better in his situation? We can imagine him, however, praying and quietly pondering God's truth during his nine months of silence. Because God humbled him by removing his ability to speak, Zechariah was able to grow in inner humility as he sought the Lord in prayer.

In his book, *The Imitation of Christ*, Thomas à Kempis wrote: "If you know how to suffer in silence, you will surely receive God's help." There are times in our lives when God allows us to go through trial and challenge, as Zechariah experienced. God often allows these circumstances in order to humble us and teach us that even in the darkest of moments, he never stops loving us. He wants to show us how trustworthy he is, even as he shows us how deeply sin has a hold on us. Such knowledge can bring us to understand our deep and constant need for his presence in our lives.

"When a humble man is brought to confusion," said Kempis, "he experiences peace because he stands firm in God and not in this world." God wants to give us the peace that comes from trust and faith in him. We receive this peace as we come to know God and stand firm in our trust of him. Like Zechariah, we should seek to rest in God's presence as we contemplate his word prayerfully. In pondering the incarnation of our Lord, we will find great peace in knowing our God has given his Son for us.

"O come, Flower of Jesse's stem, Sign of God's love for all his people: Save us without delay!"

Luke 1:26-38

26 In the sixth month the angel Gabriel was sent from God to a
city of Galilee named Nazareth, 27 to a virgin betrothed to a man
whose name was Joseph, of the house of David; and the virgin's
name was Mary. 28 And he came to her and said, "Hail, full of
grace, the Lord is with you!" 29 But she was greatly troubled at the
saying, and considered in her mind what sort of greeting this
might be. 30 And the angel said to her, "Do not be afraid, Mary, for
you have found favor with God. 31 And behold, you will conceive
in your womb and bear a son, and you shall call his name Jesus. 32
He will be great, and will be called the Son of the Most High; and
the Lord God will give to him the throne of his father David, 33
and he will reign over the house of Jacob for ever; and of his
kingdom there will be no end." 34 And Mary said to the angel,
"How shall this be, since I have no husband?" 35 And the angel
said to her, "The Holy Spirit will come upon you, and the power
of the Most High will overshadow you; therefore the child to be
born will be called holy, the Son of God. 36 And behold, your
kinswoman Elizabeth in her old age has also conceived a son; and
this is the sixth month with her who was called barren. 37 For with
God nothing will be impossible." 38 And Mary said, "Behold, I am
the handmaid of the Lord; let it be to me according to your word."
And the angel departed from her.

Presented with the seeming impossibility of conceiving a child by the power of the Holy Spirit, Mary did not stumble in her faith or try to run away from the angel Gabriel. Instead, she believed that God was capable of doing what he promised, and simply asked how it would come about. In faith, Mary relied on God and not on herself. Her "yes" to the Lord on the day that the angel visited her was the result of an entire life built upon saying "yes" to God in the small, everyday situations of her life.

In each of the important events in Mary's life, the writers of the gospels are quick to point out that Mary, though not understanding why things happened, would ponder the events in her heart. She treasured the things God did for her, and she spent time in prayer and reflection over them. As a result, her life flowed out of trust in what God had promised for her and through her son, Jesus.

Every day, we have the opportunity to imitate Mary in her love for God by pondering who he is and the marvelous promises he has given us. As we draw close to Jesus in our prayer today, we too can be empowered to say "yes" to him in our everyday situations. Every act of love and trust points to the hope we have in God's promises. Every act of faith builds the kingdom of God. We encourage one another every time we are obedient to the Lord, and every time we sit at Jesus' feet and allow him to fill us with his love.

The life of God within us cannot be hidden but manifests itself in acts of love and generosity. Mary demonstrated great faith and trust when she willingly accepted God's purposes for her. Even Zechariah, having ample time to ponder the marvels of God, was made ready to raise John to be the herald of the Messiah. At the end of his silence, he could not help but proclaim the wonders of God's plan of salvation and eagerly embrace God's purposes for his son. Let us all draw close to God and ask him for the grace to imitate Mary's "yes" to him.

Luke 1:39-45

39 In those days Mary arose and went with haste into the hill
country, to a city of Judah, 40 and she entered the house of
Zechariah and greeted Elizabeth. 41 And when Elizabeth heard
the greeting of Mary, the babe leaped in her womb; and Elizabeth
was filled with the Holy Spirit 42 and she exclaimed with a loud
cry, "Blessed are you among women, and blessed is the fruit of
your womb! 43 And why is this granted me, that the mother of
my Lord should come to me? 44 For behold, when the voice of
your greeting came to my ears, the babe in my womb leaped for
joy. 45 And blessed is she who believed that there would be a
fulfilment of what was spoken to her from the Lord."

We are all familiar with the scene that Luke paints: "When Elizabeth heard the greeting of Mary, the babe leaped in her womb" (Luke 1:41). Generations of artists have attempted to capture this visitation, seeking to convey the overwhelming, joyful hope evoked when Elizabeth voiced humanity's ageless cry to the Virgin: "Blessed are you among women, and blessed is the fruit of your womb!" (1:42).

At this singular meeting, law gives way to promise, ancient prophecy meets divine fulfillment, and the old bows to the new. Barren Elizabeth, incapable of producing life, was loved and blessed by God. And, loving him in return, she lived in anticipation, ever open to the Life-Giver. Hence, she was "filled with the Holy Spirit" (Luke 1:41) and recognized Mary as the vessel of God's salvation. Not with bitterness or envy, but with rejoicing, she acceded the higher place to Mary, "the mother of my Lord" (1:43). Content to be eclipsed, like the shadow of the old covenant by the good things of the new, she blessed Mary and all people of faith: "Blessed is she who believed . . . what was spoken to her from the Lord" (1:45).

The quiet, youthful Mary went to the aging, faithful Elizabeth to share the new things God had done. Her arrival affirmed the prayerful vigilance of Yahweh's faithful servants. In coming to celebrate her cousin's good fortune, she brought grace and abounding joy. Mary humbly accepted the honor given to her by Elizabeth and turned it immediately to the Lord whom her soul magnified.

Our God is a God of surprises, always ready to reveal himself in a new way to us. Will we refrain from embracing the new, afraid of disappointment and frustration? Or will we imitate Elizabeth and joyfully welcome the Savior Jesus who has come among us?

"Lord Jesus, we lay down all of our fear and sorrow and sin. We welcome the new life you have to offer us. 'Restore us, O God; let thy face shine, that we may be saved!'" (Psalm 80:3).

Luke 1:46-56

46 And Mary said, "My soul magnifies the Lord, 47 and my
spirit rejoices in God my Savior, 48 for he has regarded the low
estate of his handmaiden. For behold, henceforth all generations
will call me blessed; 49 for he who is mighty has done great things
for me, and holy is his name. 50 And his mercy is on those who
fear him from generation to generation. 51 He has shown strength
with his arm, he has scattered the proud in the imagination of
their hearts, 52 he has put down the mighty from their thrones,
and exalted those of low degree; 53 he has filled the hungry with
good things, and the rich he has sent empty away. 54 He has
helped his servant Israel, in remembrance of his mercy, 55 as he
spoke to our fathers, to Abraham and to his posterity for ever."
56 And Mary remained with her about three months, and
returned to her home.

My soul magnifies the Lord, and my spirit rejoices in God my Savior. (Luke 1:46-47)

Mary's hymn of praise to God echoed the rich Old Testament tradition of the Psalms and Hannah's song of praise (see 1 Samuel 2:1-10). It lifts us up to the heavenly realm as it traces salvation history up to the fulfillment of God's intention through the incarnation of his Son, Jesus.

Mary began by saying that her soul magnified the Lord: It showed his greatness and drew attention to him. How did this happen? Mary drew strength from recognizing her lowliness in light of the great might and power of God (Luke 1:48-49). By her humble recognition of the gulf between humanity and the Creator, and the depth of God's mercy in intervening in human affairs, she could be a vessel for his plan to be carried out.

The knowledge of the fulfillment of God's plan through the incarnation caused Mary's spirit to rejoice. The Greek word *agalliao* used here does not mean just to be mildly happy, but to leap for joy, to be ecstatic. Mary's heart longed for the actualization of God's promises; the prospect of their fulfillment was a source of joy to her.

The Magnificat reflects on what this fulfillment means. The Messiah's heavenly kingdom will reverse human opinions of greatness and success. The proud will be humbled and the poor exalted; those who hunger will be filled. Mary echoed the psalms, rejoicing in God's great deeds of the Old Testament—deeds of delivering his people, defeating their enemies, lifting up the lowly, and having mercy on the rejected. She also pointed to the hope in God's promised salvation. Mary saw the salvation of God actually realized in space and time through the incarnation!

Our reflection on the mysteries of the incarnation can lift our spirits to the heavenly realm. As we ponder God's work in and through his people throughout salvation history, as the Magnificat encourages us to do, a great hope will blossom in our hearts. We will yearn for the fullness of salvation with the same longing that burns in the heart of God.

"Come, King of all nations, source of your church's unity and faith: Save all mankind, your own creation!"

Luke 1:57-66

57 Now the time came for Elizabeth to be delivered, and she
gave birth to a son. 58 And her neighbors and kinsfolk heard that
the Lord had shown great mercy to her, and they rejoiced with
her. 59 And on the eighth day they came to circumcise the
child; and they would have named him Zechariah after his
father, 60 but his mother said, "Not so; he shall be called John."
61 And they said to her, "None of your kindred is called by this
name." 62 And they made signs to his father, inquiring what he
would have him called. 63 And he asked for a writing tablet, and
wrote, "His name is John." And they all marveled. 64 And
immediately his mouth was opened and his tongue loosed, and
he spoke, blessing God. 65 And fear came on all their neighbors.
And all these things were talked about through all the hill
country of Judea; 66 and all who heard them laid them up in their
hearts, saying, "What then will this child be?" For the hand of
the Lord was with him.

The name John means, "The Lord is gracious." With the birth of John to Zechariah and Elizabeth, God's grace was showered upon his people. God is gracious because the plan he announced through the prophets was being fulfilled—a plan to restore his people, to bring them life, to let his love flow freely on them. John was to herald the good news that all can have new life with the Father through Christ. This new life is a gracious gift from God; it is nothing which can be earned by our own efforts.

The people awaiting the Messiah had to be prepared for this message of the free gift. The covenant with Moses had taught them that the Almighty wanted a righteous and law-abiding people. John was called to teach the people about a Savior who would lift believers up into his own perfect goodness.

God sent John the Baptist to help "make ready for the Lord a people prepared" (Luke 1:17). John's birth prepared Zechariah's heart for the coming of Christ. Because of his own limitations, he had doubted God's messenger. By the time his child was ready to be named, his heart had been thoroughly changed. Once full of self-reliance, now he relied on God alone! This is seen clearly in the name Zechariah gave his son (1:63).

What happened in Zechariah can happen in us when we open our hearts to God's plan to raise us to the heavenlies. When John cried, "Repent, for the kingdom of heaven is at hand" (Matthew 3:2), he was asking the people to change direction. John was pleading with the people to change their minds about what pleases God. Even those of us who believe in Christ can be tempted to find solutions to our problems in our own power, determination, talent, and intelligence.

God is gracious. He wants to save us, to lift us up into his presence. He will share all things with us if we will just believe. May our hearts burn with expectation as we pray: "Come, Emmanuel, God's presence among us, our King, our Judge: Save us, Lord our God!"

Luke 1:67-80

67 And his father Zechariah was filled with the Holy Spirit, and
prophesied, saying, 68 "Blessed be the Lord God of Israel, for he
has visited and redeemed his people, 69 and has raised up a horn
of salvation for us in the house of his servant David, 70 as he spoke
by the mouth of his holy prophets from of old, 71 that we should
be saved from our enemies, and from the hand of all who hate us;
72 to perform the mercy promised to our fathers, and to remember
his holy covenant, 73 the oath which he swore to our father
Abraham, 74 to grant us that we, being delivered from the hand
of our enemies, might serve him without fear, 75 in holiness and
righteousness before him all the days of our life. 76 And you, child,
will be called the prophet of the Most High; for you will go before
the Lord to prepare his ways, 77 to give knowledge of salvation to
his people in the forgiveness of their sins, 78 through the tender
mercy of our God, when the day shall dawn upon us from on
high 79 to give light to those who sit in darkness and in the
shadow of death, to guide our feet into the way of peace." 80 And
the child grew and became strong in spirit, and he was in the
wilderness till the day of his manifestation to Israel.

Zechariah's doubts at the words of the angel brought about nine months of divinely imposed silence (see Luke 1:18-20). He had no choice; he simply could not speak. Zechariah did choose, however, to spend these months pondering God's promises and plans. Because he sat quietly in prayer, Zechariah allowed the Lord to teach him about his son John and the role he would play in salvation history.

When his tongue was finally loosed, Zechariah's actions stunned those present. They considered it odd that he would choose a name other than one from his ancestors. To Zechariah, it made perfect sense: How could he not give the boy the name the angel told him? Prayer had opened Zechariah's heart so that he could eagerly accept God's plan. No longer did it seem odd to him, but rather exciting and marvelous.

Prayer often ties things together for us. In his prophecy, Zechariah spoke of God's promise to deliver Israel from their "enemies" and was able to connect it with the forgiveness of sins that the Savior would bring. Through his prayerful silence, Zechariah came to see that the true "enemy" was sin. This was why John would arise in the power of Elijah, the ancient prophet who called Israel to repentance and obedience. Zechariah could also understand the relationship between the Savior's coming and John's role in preparing the way. John was to preach the "tender mercies" of God, so that the people's hearts would be open to receive the Savior when he appeared.

Taking time to spend with Jesus in prayer can tie many things together for us. In the midst of all the busyness we face, try to carve out a little extra time to ponder what Jesus' coming means to you. Give the Spirit the opportunity to open your heart more and reveal Jesus to you in a deeper way, just as he did for Zechariah.

"Come, Holy Spirit, and enlighten our minds to understand Jesus' coming in new and broader ways. We know that you can guide us into all truth, so we sit and await your presence."

Luke 2:1-20

1 In those days a decree went out from Caesar Augustus that
all the world should be enrolled. 2 This was the first enrollment,
when Quirini-us was governor of Syria. 3 And all went to be
enrolled, each to his own city. 4 And Joseph also went up from

Galilee, from the city of Nazareth, to Judea, to the city of David,
which is called Bethlehem, because he was of the house and
lineage of David, 5 to be enrolled with Mary, his betrothed, who
was with child. 6 And while they were there, the time came for
her to be delivered. 7 And she gave birth to her first-born son
and wrapped him in swaddling cloths, and laid him in a manger,
because there was no place for them in the inn.
8 And in that region there were shepherds out in the field,
keeping watch over their flock by night. 9 And an angel of the
Lord appeared to them, and the glory of the Lord shone around
them, and they were filled with fear. 10 And the angel said to
them, "Be not afraid; for behold, I bring you good news of a great
joy which will come to all the people; 11 for to you is born this
day in the city of David a Savior, who is Christ the Lord. 12 And
this will be a sign for you: you will find a babe wrapped in
swaddling cloths and lying in a manger." 13 And suddenly there
was with the angel a multitude of the heavenly host praising
God and saying, 14 "Glory to God in the highest, and on earth
peace among men with whom he is pleased!"
15 When the angels went away from them into heaven, the
shepherds said to one another, "Let us go over to Bethlehem and
see this thing that has happened, which the Lord has made
known to us." 16 And they went with haste, and found Mary and
Joseph, and the babe lying in a manger. 17 And when they saw it
they made known the saying which had been told them
concerning this child; 18 and all who heard it wondered at what
the shepherds told them. 19 But Mary kept all these things,
pondering them in her heart. 20 And the shepherds returned,
glorifying and praising God for all they had heard and seen, as it
had been told them.

From a Sermon by St. Augustine:

My mouth will speak the praise of the Lord, of the Lord through whom all things have been made and who has been made in the midst of all things; who is the Revealer of his Father, the Creator of his mother; who is . . . the Word of God before all time, the Word made flesh at a suitable time. Maker of the sun, He is made under the sun. Disposer of all ages in the bosom of the Father, he consecrates this day in the womb of his mother. . . . Creator of heaven and earth, he was born on earth, under heaven. Unspeakably wise, he is wisely speechless; filling the world, he lies in a manger; Ruler of the stars, he nurses at his mother's bosom.

"He is both great in the nature of God, and small in the form of a servant, but in such a way that his greatness is not diminished by his smallness, nor his smallness overwhelmed by his greatness. For he did not desert his divine works when he took to himself human members. Nor did he cease to reach from end to end mightily, and to order all things sweetly, when, having put on the infirmity of the flesh, he was conceived into the Virgin's womb.

"Let no one, therefore, believe that the Son of God was changed or transformed into the Son of man; but rather let us believe that he, remaining the Son of God, was made the Son of man, without loss of his divine substance, and by a perfect assumption of the human substance. Nor do the words, 'The Word was God,' and 'The Word was made flesh,' signify that the Word was made flesh in such a way that it ceased to be God; for in the flesh itself, because the Word was made flesh, 'Emmanuel, God with us,' was born.

"Let the world, therefore, rejoice in those who believe. To save them, he came through whom the world was made—the Creator of Mary, born of Mary; the Son of David, Lord of David; the seed of Abraham, who was before Abraham; the Maker of the earth, made on the earth; he who brought the heavens into existence, brought into existence under the heavens. He himself is the day which the Lord has made, and the day of our heart is itself the Lord. Let us walk in his light, let us rejoice and take delight in it."

Luke 2:21-40

21 And at the end of eight days, when he was circumcised, he
was called Jesus, the name given by the angel before he was
conceived in the womb.
22 And when the time came for their purification according to
the law of Moses, they brought him up to Jerusalem to present
him to the Lord 23 (as it is written in the law of the Lord, "Every
male that opens the womb shall be called holy to the Lord")
24 and to offer a sacrifice according to what is said in the law of
the Lord, "a pair of turtledoves, or two young pigeons." 25 Now
there was a man in Jerusalem, whose name was Simeon, and this
man was righteous and devout, looking for the consolation of
Israel, and the Holy Spirit was upon him. 26 And it had been
revealed to him by the Holy Spirit that he should not see death
before he had seen the Lord's Christ. 27 And inspired by the
Spirit he came into the temple; and when the parents brought in
the child Jesus, to do for him according to the custom of the law,
28 he took him up in his arms and blessed God and said, 29 "Lord,
now lettest thou thy servant depart in peace, according to thy
word; 30 for mine eyes have seen thy salvation 31 which thou
hast prepared in the presence of all peoples, 32 a light for
revelation to the Gentiles, and for glory to thy people Israel."
33 And his father and his mother marveled at what was said
about him; 34 and Simeon blessed them and said to Mary his
mother, "Behold, this child is set for the fall and rising of many
in Israel, and for a sign that is spoken against 35 (and a sword

will pierce through your own soul also), that thoughts out of
many hearts may be revealed."
36 And there was a prophetess, Anna, the daughter of Phanu-
el, of the tribe of Asher; she was of a great age, having lived with
her husband seven years from her virginity, 37 and as a widow till
she was eighty-four. She did not depart from the temple,
worshiping with fasting and prayer night and day. 38 And
coming up at that very hour she gave thanks to God, and spoke
of him to all who were looking for the redemption of Jerusalem.
39 And when they had performed everything according to the law
of the Lord, they returned into Galilee, to their own city,
Nazareth. 40 And the child grew and became strong, filled with
wisdom; and the favor of God was upon him.

What did Simeon and Anna expect to find as they prayed in the temple and fasted for the coming of the Messiah? Were they surprised that the answer to their supplications was a tiny baby, helpless and dependent on his humble parents? Could this little child really be the "King of glory" whom the psalmist had proclaimed (see Psalm 24:8-10)? Here was God incarnate, taking on our own flesh in the most humble way possible. "He had to be made like his brethren in every respect, so that he might become a merciful and faithful high priest in the service of God" (see Hebrews 2:17).

This passage is read on the Feast of the Presentation of Jesus in the temple, also known as the "Feast of the Encounter." The term "encounter" suggests an element of surprise. All their lives, Simeon and Anna had prepared themselves for this encounter in the temple, even though they didn't know when or how it would happen. Because of their prayer and attentiveness to the Spirit, these two people were able to see the splendor of God in Mary's small child. Filled with gratitude, Simeon "took him up in his arms and blessed God" (Luke 2:28).

How blessed are we that the resurrected Lord has come to his temple to remain! In the Eucharist, under the appearance of ordinary bread and wine, Jesus comes to meet us. In baptism, he has taken up residence in the temple of our hearts as well. By the shedding of his blood and the outpouring of his Spirit, he has purified us and delivered us from death (see Malachi 3:2-3).

Like Simeon and Anna, let us prepare ourselves for our encounter with the Lord. We may be surprised to meet him in those around us, in the poor and helpless, the sick and dying. He is always waiting for us in his temple, in the Eucharist, waiting for us to embrace him and hold him close to our hearts. His love—stronger than any sin we may commit—will purify us. Then like Simeon, we will be filled with his peace (Luke 2:29). Like Anna, we will give "thanks to God" (2:38).

Luke 2:41-52

[41] Now his parents went to Jerusalem every year at the feast of
the Passover. [42] And when he was twelve years old, they went up
according to custom; [43] and when the feast was ended, as they
were returning, the boy Jesus stayed behind in Jerusalem. His
parents did not know it, [44] but supposing him to be in the
company they went a day's journey, and they sought him among
their kinsfolk and acquaintances; [45] and when they did not find
him, they returned to Jerusalem, seeking him. [46] After three days
they found him in the temple, sitting among the teachers,
listening to them and asking them questions; [47] and all who heard
him were amazed at his understanding and his answers. [48] And
when they saw him they were astonished; and his mother said to

him, "Son, why have you treated us so? Behold, your father and I have been looking for you anxiously." 49 And he said to them, "How is it that you sought me? Did you not know that I must be in my Father's house?" 50 And they did not understand the saying which he spoke to them. 51 And he went down with them and came to Nazareth, and was obedient to them; and his mother kept all these things in her heart. 52 And Jesus increased in wisdom and in stature, and in favor with God and man.

The Christian family is often described as a mini-church, and is intended by God to exhibit all the characteristics of the whole body of Christ. There is much to be learned by pondering this fact in our hearts and asking God questions about what it means for our families today to be mini-churches. All parents are individually called by God to play a special role in forming and sustaining the mini-church of their family.

As we look at the example of the Holy Family in this passage, we can see at least two characteristics we in our families are called to embrace and exhibit: obedience to and love for God. This passage illustrates how Mary and Joseph cultivated these qualities in the spiritual life of their family.

They were obedient to the Jewish law by going every year to Jerusalem—a long journey by foot from Nazareth—for the Feast of the Passover (Luke 2:41). According to the ordinances given by God to his people, the Jews were to observe Passover each year. In obedience to the command of God and in love for him, the Holy Family participated in this celebration, even going to Jerusalem for it. It is clear that Joseph and Mary loved God and honored him by being obedient to his ordinances and in their obedience to God set the example for Jesus.

The Holy Family was obviously a place where there was a deep love of God; it was a place where the scriptures and the things of God were discussed and honored. This is suggested by Jesus being found in the temple asking and answering questions of the teachers in the temple: "All who heard him were amazed at his understanding and his answers" (Luke 2:47). Mary and Joseph had evidently taught him well; their example of love and obedience paved the way for Jesus to be open to all his heavenly Father would teach him.

Families today would greatly profit by studying and following the example set by the Holy Family. They show how the family can truly be a mini-church and reflect all that should be part of the larger body of Christ. Let us reflect on the love and obedience shown by the Holy Family and strive to follow their example. Even if we do not always understand, we can ask God for the grace to love him and be obedient to him.

A Devotional Commentary on Luke

Preparations for Jesus' Ministry

LUKE
3–4:13

Luke 3:1-6

1 In the fifteenth year of the reign of Tiberi-us Caesar, Pontius
Pilate being governor of Judea, and Herod being tetrarch of
Galilee, and his brother Philip tetrarch of the region of Ituraea
and Trachonitis, and Lysani-as tetrarch of Abilene, 2 in the high-
priesthood of Annas and Caiaphas, the word of God came to
John the son of Zechariah in the wilderness; 3 and he went into
all the region about the Jordan, preaching a baptism of
repentance for the forgiveness of sins. 4 As it is written in the
book of the words of Isaiah the prophet, "The voice of one
crying in the wilderness: Prepare the way of the Lord, make his
paths straight. 5 Every valley shall be filled, and every mountain
and hill shall be brought low, and the crooked shall be made
straight, and the rough ways shall be made smooth; 6 and all flesh
shall see the salvation of God."

As he told the story of Jesus' coming as a man, Luke took particular care to identify a specific point in history when these events unfolded. He noted who was in power, where they ruled, and when it all occurred. He also stated explicitly that the word of God came to one particular person—John—who preached a distinct message rooted in his people's prophetic heritage.

By crafting his gospel in this way, Luke emphasized a very important point: God speaks to his people, through his word, in the real world. He bridges the gap between heaven and earth, and as a result, lives are changed forever.

How easy it is to lose sight of the fact that God acts each and every day! Like the faithful Jewish believers of Jesus' time, we may take scripture very seriously and still fail to recognize God when he reveals himself. Hoping that God will act in the future, we look for the new heaven and new earth that will come at the end of time. But we should remember that the Jews—God's own chosen people—believed they too would recognize the Messiah, yet most did not. Even we Christians, by definition "believers in Christ," can be skeptical when we hear of miraculous happenings throughout the world.

How can we recognize God's action today? We can hold on to the things God has revealed already, and always remember that God wants to teach us even more with each new day. He is ever at work, advancing his plan toward its fulfillment. As it was in the days of John the Baptist, so it is in our day. Any work that brings down the mountains of sin and exalts the lowly and humble of heart is part of God's plan to prepare his way. God loves us deeply; he is always seeking to bring us to himself, smoothing out the "rough ways" in our hearts that keep us from advancing on the path to his love.

"Come, Lord Jesus, and 'prepare the way' in us so that we can receive you more fully. Open our hearts to your word, and show us, in specific, unmistakable ways, how you are at work today. Lord, show us your salvation."

Luke 3:7-20

7 He said therefore to the multitudes that came out to be
baptized by him, "You brood of vipers! Who warned you to flee
from the wrath to come? 8 Bear fruits that befit repentance, and
do not begin to say to yourselves, 'We have Abraham as our
father'; for I tell you, God is able from these stones to raise up
children to Abraham. 9 Even now the axe is laid to the root of
the trees; every tree therefore that does not bear good fruit is cut
down and thrown into the fire."
10 And the multitudes asked him, "What then shall we do?"

11 And he answered them, "He who has two coats, let him share
with him who has none; and he who has food, let him do
likewise." 12 Tax collectors also came to be baptized, and said to
him, "Teacher, what shall we do?" 13 And he said to them,
"Collect no more than is appointed you." 14 Soldiers also asked
him, "And we, what shall we do?" And he said to them, "Rob no
one by violence or by false accusation, and be content with
your wages."
15 As the people were in expectation, and all men questioned
in their hearts concerning John, whether perhaps he were the
Christ, 16 John answered them all, "I baptize you with water; but
he who is mightier than I is coming, the thong of whose sandals
I am not worthy to untie; he will baptize you with the Holy
Spirit and with fire. 17 His winnowing fork is in his hand, to
clear his threshing floor, and to gather the wheat into his
granary, but the chaff he will burn with unquenchable fire."
18 So, with many other exhortations, he preached good news to
the people. 19 But Herod the tetrarch, who had been reproved by
him for Herodi-as, his brother's wife, and for all the evil things
that Herod had done, 20 added this to them all, that he shut up
John in prison.

John the Baptist had just given the multitudes, the tax collectors, and soldiers his latest pronouncement, telling them to be generous with others, to shape up their business practices, and to be content with their pay: "He who has two coats, let him share with him who has none; and he who has food, let him do likewise." "Collect no more than is appointed you." "Rob no one by violence or by false accusation, and be content with your wages" (Luke 3:11,13,14). Luke says that John often preached this way, and he described these exhortations as "good news" (3:18).

Many of us find John's words to be hard and demanding, at least in part. How then is it that John's preaching is "good news"? At the heart of what John said here and on other occasions is the recognition that Jesus had come to save us and cleanse us from sin, and to give us life in the Holy Spirit: "I baptize you with water; but he who is mightier than I is coming . . . ; he will baptize you with the Holy Spirit and with fire" (Luke 3:16). John's words spoke of salvation and true life.

When we begin to understand the spiritual life Jesus came to give us, we also begin to see why the gospel is good news even though it challenges us to change our lives. As we start to experience the life Christ has for us, we will begin to want to live out exhortations like John the Baptist's. We won't be trying to live righteously just to avoid punishment. No, we will see sin and living for self as burdens we do not want to carry, and we will entrust ourselves to the life God has for us.

When we begin to experience the good news of salvation in our hearts, we will understand the words of Paul: "The peace of God, which passes all understanding, will keep your hearts and your minds in Christ Jesus" (Philippians 4:7). And as we understand these words, we will naturally "rejoice in the Lord always" (4:4), even as we are growing in our desire and ability to be true and generous as John the Baptist directed the people long ago. As we are in Christ and his love, we will know why John's words are truly good news.

Luke 3:21-22

21 Now when all the people were baptized, and when Jesus also
had been baptized and was praying, the heaven was opened,
22 and the Holy Spirit descended upon him in bodily form, as a

dove, and a voice came from heaven, "Thou art my beloved Son; with thee I am well pleased."

Thou art my Son, the Beloved; with you I am well pleased. (Luke 3:22)

These words were heard at Jesus' baptism, when he began his public ministry. They might more poignantly have been repeated at the end of that ministry, when Jesus "breathed his last" (Luke 23:46). The point is that throughout his life Jesus was beloved of the Father and pleased him.

That is why not only the New Testament but the Old as well point to Jesus and look to him. When Peter first preached to Cornelius, he proclaimed Jesus' lordship over all—his anointing with the Holy Spirit and with power (see Acts 10:36-38). But long before Peter, the prophet Isaiah had eloquently pointed to the Messiah as God's chosen one in whom he delighted (see Isaiah 42:1).

We too need to look to Jesus and to center our lives on him and learn who he is. Too often we center on ourselves, even in our spirituality, seeking to become better, more holy, more joyful. But the Father's joy rested on Jesus; the Spirit's joy is to teach us who Jesus is. Jesus is truly and fully human, and truly and fully divine. In his humanity, he is what we are to become—fully alive, fully open to God, fully realizing our potential as beings created in the image and likeness of God.

John the Baptist knew that Jesus was different, but it took the Holy Spirit to teach him that "this is the Son of God" (John 1:34). The disciples spent years with him, only gradually realizing what made Jesus so different from them in thought, word, and action. It was only after the Holy Spirit came upon them at Pentecost that they were able to begin preaching who Jesus truly is.

As the Holy Spirit descended upon Jesus at his baptism, let us pray that he will descend upon us anew today, that he will deepen the revelation of Jesus as the Beloved in whom the Father and the Holy Spirit delight. Let us ask the Spirit of God to enroll us in the school of Christ so we may learn from him. May we seek to diminish, so that Christ may increase in us; and when the Father looks at us, may he see a people who have become like his Son, and declare himself well pleased.

Luke 3:23-38

23 Jesus, when he began his ministry, was about thirty years of
age, being the son (as was supposed) of Joseph, the son of Heli,
24 the son of Matthat, the son of Levi, the son of Melchi, the son
of Janna-i, the son of Joseph, 25 the son of Mattathias, the son of
Amos, the son of Nahum, the son of Esli, the son of Naggai,
26 the son of Maath, the son of Mattathias, the son of Seme-in,
the son of Josech, the son of Joda, 27 the son of Jo-anan, the son
of Rhesa, the son of Zerubbabel, the son of She-alti-el, the son of
Neri, 28 the son of Melchi, the son of Addi, the son of Cosam,
the son of Elmadam, the son of Er, 29 the son of Joshua, the son
of Eliezer, the son of Jorim, the son of Matthat, the son of Levi,
30 the son of Simeon, the son of Judah, the son of Joseph, the son
of Jonam, the son of Eliakim, 31 the son of Mele-a, the son of
Menna, the son of Mattatha, the son of Nathan, the son of
David, 32 the son of Jesse, the son of Obed, the son of Boaz, the
son of Sala, the son of Nahshon, 33 the son of Amminadab, the
son of Admin, the son of Arni, the son of Hezron, the son of
Perez, the son of Judah, 34 the son of Jacob, the son of Isaac, the
son of Abraham, the son of Terah, the son of Nahor,
35 the son of Serug, the son of Reu, the son of Peleg, the son of

Eber, the son of Shelah,
36 the son of Ca-inan, the son of
Arphaxad, the son of Shem, the son of Noah, the son of
Lamech,
37 the son of Methuselah, the son of Enoch, the son of
Jared, the son of Mahalale-el, the son of Ca-inan,
38 the son of
Enos, the son of Seth, the son of Adam, the son of God.

Jesus was thirty years old when he began his public ministry. As he waited on his Father to reveal to him when he should begin the work he was sent to do, he lived a quiet, humble life with his family in Nazareth.

During these years, Jesus probably worked at his earthly father's trade of carpentry, studied, and prayed. Like us in all things except sin, he experienced the daily routines of life much as we do. Sharing our humanity, he lived our own struggles and triumphs. He got up each morning, worked through the day, ate with his family, and went to bed. He laughed and he cried. Even though he was the Son of God, he shared our own earthly existence.

Luke shows us just how rooted Jesus was in humanity by presenting his genealogy. Such listings were important to the Jews. Genealogies were kept in public records. In order to become a priest, a man had to prove an unbroken descent from Aaron, the first Hebrew priest. Priests could lose their office if they could not produce their genealogy (see Ezra 2:62).

The author of Hebrews proclaims Jesus as "a great high priest who has passed through the heavens" (Hebrews 4:14). And yet, because he lived a human life, Christ is "not a high priest who is unable to sympathize with our weaknesses, but one who in every respect has been tempted as we are, yet without sinning" (4:15). We can take great comfort in this, and "draw near to the throne of grace, that we may receive mercy" (4:16).

Unlike the genealogy in the Gospel of Matthew (see 1:1-17), Luke's genealogy traces Jesus' heritage beyond Abraham, the father of the Jewish nation, all the way to Adam, the father of the human race. In this way, Luke shows us that Jesus is not just the high priest for the Israelites, but for all humanity. He is the Savior to all people, in all times, and for all nations. His redeeming grace knows no bounds. He excludes no one.

"Father, thank you for your plan of salvation. You sent your only begotten Son into human history, to bring humanity back to you. He is the high priest, whom we can approach with confidence because he was made one like us. Father, your mercy is everlasting. We praise you for your kindness and love."

Luke 4:1-13

1 And Jesus, full of the Holy Spirit, returned from the Jordan,
and was led by the Spirit 2 for forty days in the wilderness,
tempted by the devil. And he ate nothing in those days; and
when they were ended, he was hungry. 3 The devil said to him,
"If you are the Son of God, command this stone to become
bread." 4 And Jesus answered him, "It is written, 'Man shall not
live by bread alone.' " 5 And the devil took him up, and showed
him all the kingdoms of the world in a moment of time, 6 and
said to him, "To you I will give all this authority and their glory;
for it has been delivered to me, and I give it to whom I will.
7 If you, then, will worship me, it shall all be yours." 8 And Jesus
answered him, "It is written, 'You shall worship the Lord your
God, and him only shall you serve.' " 9 And he took him to
Jerusalem, and set him on the pinnacle of the temple, and said to
him, "If you are the Son of God, throw yourself down from here;
10 for it is written, 'He will give his angels charge of you, to guard

you,' 11 and 'On their hands they will bear you up, lest you
strike your foot against a stone.'" 12 And Jesus answered him, "It
is said, 'You shall not tempt the Lord your God.'" 13 And when
the devil had ended every temptation, he departed from him
until an opportune time.

Until Jesus came among us as a man, no one—not even the most beloved prophets of God—had succeeded in resisting all temptation and following the Lord's commands perfectly. So, how did Jesus succeed where so many others had failed? It is easy to think of him as special because he was God's Son, yet scripture tells us that he was like us in every way, except that he did not sin (see Hebrews 4:15).

After he was baptized by John in the Jordan River, Jesus was led to a face-to-face confrontation with Satan. In obedience to the Spirit, Jesus actually took the offensive against temptation instead of avoiding it! Here, at the very beginning of his ministry, he attacked the power of Satan with the word of God, the "sword of the Spirit" (Ephesians 6:17). And, for forty days in the Judean wilderness, Jesus remained steadfast, relying solely on his Father's promises.

Think of how, during those forty days, Jesus relived his people's history. Like his ancestors—who spent forty years in the desert—Jesus was tempted to relate to God on merely human terms or to abandon him altogether. However, where the Israelites failed, Jesus succeeded. He lived "in the shadow of the Almighty," and the Lord was his "refuge" (Psalm 91:1-2).

Thanks be to God that Jesus has come! He has reversed the pattern of sinful humanity, freeing us from bondage to sin and death! Today, because of Jesus, we can know the same victory he knew. Because we have received his Spirit, we can face times of temptation patiently, relying on the power of God within us. Should we fail, we have the precious gift of repentance, which restores us immediately to God's love and protection. By imitating Jesus' humility and trust in the Father, we can learn to stand our ground and share in his triumph.

"Holy Spirit, fill us with your power and word so that we can resist temptation. Make us more like Jesus, obedient children who please their heavenly Father."

A New Way Is Revealed

Luke
4:14–6:49

Luke 4:14-30

[14] And Jesus returned in the power of the Spirit into Galilee,
and a report concerning him went out through all the
surrounding country. [15] And he taught in their synagogues, being
glorified by all.
[16] And he came to Nazareth, where he had been brought up;
and he went to the synagogue, as his custom was, on the sabbath
day. And he stood up to read; [17] and there was given to him the
book of the prophet Isaiah. He opened the book and found the
place where it was written, [18] "The Spirit of the Lord is upon
me, because he has anointed me to preach good news to the
poor. He has sent me to proclaim release to the captives and
recovering of sight to the blind, to set at liberty those who are
oppressed, [19] to proclaim the acceptable year of the Lord."
[20] And he closed the book, and gave it back to the attendant,
and sat down; and the eyes of all in the synagogue were fixed on
him. [21] And he began to say to them, "Today this scripture has
been fulfilled in your hearing." [22] And all spoke well of him, and
wondered at the gracious words which proceeded out of his
mouth; and they said, "Is not this Joseph's son?" [23] And he said
to them, "Doubtless you will quote to me this proverb,
'Physician, heal yourself; what we have heard you did at
Caperna-um, do here also in your own country.' " [24] And he said,
"Truly, I say to you, no prophet is acceptable in his own country.
[25] But in truth, I tell you, there were many widows in Israel in
the days of Elijah, when the heaven was shut up three years and
six months, when there came a great famine over all the land;
[26] and Elijah was sent to none of them but only to Zarephath, in
the land of Sidon, to a woman who was a widow. [27] And there
were many lepers in Israel in the time of the prophet Elisha; and
none of them was cleansed, but only Naaman the Syrian."
[28] When they heard this, all in the synagogue were filled with
wrath. [29] And they rose up and put him out of the city, and led

him to the brow of the hill on which their city was built, that they might throw him down headlong. 30 But passing through the midst of them he went away.

In our presence today, Jesus continues to fulfill the prophecy to "preach good news to the poor" and provide "release to the captives" (Luke 4:18; see Isaiah 61:1-4). We know that Jesus is the Messiah, the "anointed one," sent to fulfill all of God's promises. But imagine yourself as one of those in the synagogue in Nazareth, hearing Jesus first announce that these words were being fulfilled right before their eyes. You probably would have thought: "How can I really be released from sin, or be freed from guilt and hopelessness? When was the last time I felt favored by anyone, let alone by God?"

To an Israelite of Jesus' time, the "acceptable year of the Lord" referred to the Jubilee year described in Leviticus 25. Every fiftieth year, all debts were to be remitted and all slaves set free; everyone in Israel was called to celebrate and to rest, to enjoy the fruits of six years of harvest. Thanks to Jesus, the debt of sin can be lifted from us every day; slavery to old ways can be removed at any time through his Spirit. We can all rejoice as we hear these words!

The fact that Jesus' ministry was accepted for the most part by the outcasts of society, even by unbelieving Gentiles, threatened some of his "godly" listeners, and aroused murderous thoughts among them. Among the Nazarenes, the fact that Jesus was so popular outside of his hometown was hard to accept: Why should Capernaum get all the miracles (Luke 4:24)? Yet Jesus didn't let such hostility deter him from accomplishing his mission. This was only the beginning of the opposition he would face as he made his way toward his destiny in Jerusalem.

We may think sometimes that Jesus actually liked stirring up controversy. He must have known that his words would not always go down easily, but he never tried to soften them. The fact is that Jesus does want to shake us up so that he can get our attention. He came to proclaim a "good news" unlike anything we might expect, and if we are to listen properly, we will need to be made uncomfortable. How else will we want to part with sin and follow him on the way to the cross?

"Lord Jesus, today you offer us a choice: to accept your words, or to listen to the desires of our fallen nature. Help us to be generous recipients of your grace and instruments of your peace."

Luke 4:31-37

[31] And he went down to Caperna-um, a city of Galilee. And
he was teaching them on the sabbath; [32] and they were
astonished at his teaching, for his word was with authority.
[33] And in the synagogue there was a man who had the spirit of
an unclean demon; and he cried out with a loud voice, [34] "Ah!
What have you to do with us, Jesus of Nazareth? Have you come
to destroy us? I know who you are, the Holy One of God." [35] But
Jesus rebuked him, saying, "Be silent, and come out of him!"
And when the demon had thrown him down in the midst, he
came out of him, having done him no harm. [36] And they were all
amazed and said to one another, "What is this word? For with
authority and power he commands the unclean spirits, and they
come out." [37] And reports of him went out into every place in
the surrounding region.

What quality was it in that particular teacher that enabled him or her to lead you on to excellence? What was it about that special person who inspired in you attentiveness and responsibility? Perhaps your father had it, or your mother. It's called authority, and we can see from Luke that Jesus definitely had it in a unique way. "They were astounded at his teaching, for his word was with authority" (Luke 4:32).

To the people of Capernaum, Jesus was astonishing because through his words, he was opening them to the thoughts of the Father. He was not just repackaging familiar human wisdom in a new and provocative way. No—his words were helping them to encounter God. Because of his unique identity, Jesus knew the deepest thoughts and desires of God. Our Lord was an original thinker, and his words confronted the earthly minds of the people and brought them into contact with God's inmost desires. His authority came from above because he himself was from above. The people could place their hopes in his words with confidence.

But if his words revealed his identity, so too did his actions. He used his authority and power to overcome the forces of evil and to restore his people to wholeness. We see that he had the authority to force an evil spirit to obey him against his will. Jesus rebuked the demon and ordered him to leave the man. Through his authority and power, Jesus won the victory! (Luke 4:35-36).

Jesus' desire to defeat the Evil One is no stronger than his longing to heal us—men and women who are in bondage to sin. Our weak hearts are attached to our earthly ways of thinking; they resist his new life. Through repentance, turning away from the sin in our lives and turning toward Jesus, we too can experience wholeness. Like the man with the unclean spirit, we can trust Jesus to cleanse our hearts and minds and fill us with new life. Today, let's be clear that through the Spirit, Jesus is present among us and within us and that we can meet him as we turn our hearts to him in prayer.

"Lord Jesus, open our minds and our hearts to your power and authority. We reject those interests that lead us away from you and ask you to renew our minds and revive our love for you."

Luke 4:38-44

38 And he arose and left the synagogue, and entered Simon's
house. Now Simon's mother-in-law was ill with a high fever,
and they besought him for her. 39 And he stood over her and
rebuked the fever, and it left her; and immediately she rose and
served them. 40 Now when the sun was setting, all those who had
any that were sick with various diseases brought them to him;
and he laid his hands on every one of them and healed them. 41
And demons also came out of many, crying, "You are the Son of
God!" But he rebuked them, and would not allow them to speak,
because they knew that he was the Christ. 42 And when it was
day he departed and went into a lonely place. And the people
sought him and came to him, and would have kept him from
leaving them; 43 but he said to them, "I must preach the good
news of the kingdom of God to the other cities also; for I was
sent for this purpose." 44 And he was preaching in the synagogues
of Judea.

What a triumphant day it had been! Jesus began that sabbath by making a deep impression on the people of Capernaum, teaching with authority and then curing a man possessed by a demon. He then returned to Simon Peter's house, where he healed Simon's mother-in-law. And that evening, crowds of sick and demon-possessed people thronged to Jesus, who attended to each one, healing and delivering them. Truly Jesus had come to "proclaim the acceptable year of the Lord" (Luke 4:19).

It is no surprise that the people of Capernaum wanted Jesus to remain with them and continue his ministry. But instead of holding on to the comfort of recognition and acclaim, Jesus chose to leave so that he could continue preaching the gospel in other cities. The popular approval he received in Capernaum held no more sway over him than his earlier rejection in Nazareth. As the one anointed by God with the Spirit and sent to proclaim the good news to all people, Jesus would not settle for recognition as a wonder-worker. He was compelled by the Spirit living in him to do no less than establish the kingdom of God on earth.

By piling up stories of healing and deliverance one after another, Luke shows us how Jesus is constantly at work. Through his ministry, Jesus never stopped working—not only performing wonderful healings, but forgiving people's sins and revealing God the Father to them. He always sought to reach more and more people, calling them to conversion of heart and a deeper relationship with his Father.

Now ascended in glory and seated at the Father's right hand, Jesus continues his work of advancing his kingdom in this world. As members of his body on earth, we continue to receive his ministry of healing, deliverance, and forgiveness. Jesus never stops calling us into a deeper life with him and bestowing on us progressive growth in holiness, wisdom for our lives, power over sin, and love for one another. Let us not be content with a small portion, but follow him wholeheartedly. Let us open our hearts to his life-giving power and love.

"Lord Jesus, open us up to the fullness of the blessings of your kingdom. Let your word bring life to us and reveal your purposes. We want to respond deeply to your grace."

Luke 5:1-11

1 While the people pressed upon him to hear the word of God,
he was standing by the lake of Gennesaret. 2 And he saw two
boats by the lake; but the fishermen had gone out of them and

were washing their nets. 3 Getting into one of the boats, which
was Simon's, he asked him to put out a little from the land. And
he sat down and taught the people from the boat. 4 And when
he had ceased speaking, he said to Simon, "Put out into the deep
and let down your nets for a catch." 5 And Simon answered,
"Master, we toiled all night and took nothing! But at your word I
will let down the nets." 6 And when they had done this, they
enclosed a great shoal of fish; and as their nets were breaking,
7 they beckoned to their partners in the other boat to come and
help them. And they came and filled both the boats, so that they
began to sink. 8 But when Simon Peter saw it, he fell down at
Jesus' knees, saying, "Depart from me, for I am a sinful man, O
Lord." 9 For he was astonished, and all that were with him, at
the catch of fish which they had taken; 10 and so also were James
and John, sons of Zebedee, who were partners with Simon. And
Jesus said to Simon, "Do not be afraid; henceforth you will be
catching men." 11 And when they had brought their boats to
land, they left everything and followed him.

Upon Jesus' command, Simon dropped his nets into the sea and hauled out a colossal shoal of fish. The enormous catch stunned Simon, who had caught nothing the previous night. In the face of such a miracle, Simon realized he was in the presence of the Lord, and he knew the Lord could see his sin. Humbled and frightened by this realization, Simon fell to his knees in repentance. But Jesus said, "Do not be afraid; henceforth you will be catching men" (Luke 5:10).

Like Simon Peter, the prophet Isaiah also had a revelation of the Lord that humbled and terrified him: "Woe is me! For I am lost . . . for my eyes have seen . . . the Lord" (Isaiah 6:5). However, the touch of a burning coal from the altar cleansed him of his sins and freed him from all guilt. Once purified, Isaiah was able to hear the cry of the Lord's heart: "Whom shall I send? And who will go for us?" Without hesitation, Isaiah called out, "Here am I! Send me!" (6:8).

God longs to commission each of us, just as he commissioned Peter and Isaiah. As we allow God to overwhelm us with his love, we too will hear the call to discipleship. We will know that we are unworthy of such an honor, but we will also know that, through repentance, we can be empowered by the Spirit to intercede, to forgive, and to proclaim the gospel.

As our relationship with Jesus deepens, so too will our love for him and, like Peter and Isaiah, we will want to forsake everything for God. Let us not be afraid to humble ourselves before the Lord and receive the commission he has for us. There is no greater honor than to be a servant of the Lord, equipped to "catch" souls for his kingdom.

"Lord Jesus, cleanse our sin and empower us with your presence. Here we are, Lord! Send us! Empower us to advance your kingdom! Teach us to speak your words and minister your love to everyone we meet."

Luke 5:12-16

12 While he was in one of the cities, there came a man full of
leprosy; and when he saw Jesus, he fell on his face and besought
him, "Lord, if you will, you can make me clean." 13 And he
stretched out his hand, and touched him, saying, "I will; be
clean." And immediately the leprosy left him. 14 And he charged
him to tell no one; but "go and show yourself to the priest, and
make an offering for your cleansing, as Moses commanded, for a
proof to the people." 15 But so much the more the report went
abroad concerning him; and great multitudes gathered to hear

and to be healed of their infirmities. [16] But he withdrew to the wilderness and prayed.

Because they carried the stigma of ritual defilement, lepers and victims of other virulent skin diseases were forced to live in squalid quarantined conditions in Jesus' time. We can only imagine the terrible psychological and emotional burden these people must have carried.

Sin is a spiritual disease that results in its own type of "quarantine." It separates us from one another and alienates us from God. Like physical disease, it not only affects our bodies but our minds as well. Similarly, it can infect other members of the body of Christ. Ultimately, if not attended to, this condition can lead to eternal death.

With great compassion and love, Jesus came into the world to offer his healing touch. Risking defilement and disease himself, he reached out to the sick and the outcast and cleansed them. Every time Jesus touched someone and removed that person's sickness or burden, he foreshadowed the time when he would bear all our griefs and carry all our sorrows on the cross, winning redemption for God's people (see Isaiah 53:4,10-12).

In Jesus, we too can be changed from unclean to clean, from sickness to health, from death to life, from the darkness of sin to the radiance of God's presence. Jesus came to heal us by "the washing of regeneration and renewal in the Holy Spirit" (Titus 3:5). The blood that poured out from his side has the power to bring us healing even today as we cry out, "Lord, if you will, you can make me clean" (Luke 5:12).

In Christ we no longer need to suffer the wounds of hatred, anger, and envy. We can be cured of infectious and contagious sins like malice and slander. We do not have to be driven by fear or controlled by guilt. Jesus forgives us and offers us peace and a new life in him. Clothed with righteousness, we can walk in his light, even with those from whom we had once been alienated. What a message of hope!

Speaking in the name of the Lord, Ezekiel prophesied: "I will sprinkle clean water upon you, and you shall be clean from all your uncleannesses. . . . A new heart I will give you, and a new spirit I will put within you" (Ezekiel 36:25-26). Let us turn to Jesus in faith and allow him to cleanse us.

Luke 5:17-26

17 On one of those days, as he was teaching, there were
Pharisees and teachers of the law sitting by, who had come from
every village of Galilee and Judea and from Jerusalem; and the
power of the Lord was with him to heal. 18 And behold, men
were bringing on a bed a man who was paralyzed, and they
sought to bring him in and lay him before Jesus; 19 but finding
no way to bring him in, because of the crowd, they went up on
the roof and let him down with his bed through the tiles into the
midst before Jesus. 20 And when he saw their faith he said,
"Man, your sins are forgiven you." 21 And the scribes and the
Pharisees began to question, saying, "Who is this that speaks
blasphemies? Who can forgive sins but God only?" 22 When
Jesus perceived their questionings, he answered them, "Why do
you question in your hearts? 23 Which is easier, to say, 'Your sins
are forgiven you,' or to say, 'Rise and walk'? 24 But that you may
know that the Son of man has authority on earth to forgive
sins"—he said to the man who was paralyzed—"I say to you, rise,
take up your bed and go home." 25 And immediately he rose

before them, and took up that on which he lay, and went home, glorifying God. 26 And amazement seized them all, and they glorified God and were filled with awe, saying, "We have seen strange things today."

The work Jesus came to do was to forgive sin and to restore us to the Father. While on earth, Jesus always pointed to the Father's will behind the actions he performed. Although the full restoration will only occur when Jesus returns in glory, Jesus performs the work of the Father even now as a sign of the coming of the kingdom. Until he comes in glory, we taste the first fruits of the full harvest to come through the Holy Spirit who dwells in us.

Because at the dawn of history humanity abused its liberty and sin entered the world, all people inherited the effects of sin—sickness, death, and evil. Jesus not only forgave the paralytic, but healed him by going to the root cause of his disease—namely sin. Before his healing, the paralytic lay helpless and hopeless on his mat. He was unable to overcome this condition on his own; he relied on his friends to lower him down to Jesus. His friends had seen Jesus work before and knew that anyone who came face to face with Jesus was never the same again.

After he was forgiven and healed, the paralytic was able to stand up and to walk. More importantly, because he had been touched by Jesus, he could stand in a right relationship to God; he could walk freely in the newness of life.

Only God has the power to forgive sin. Consequently, the scribes and Pharisees saw it as blasphemy when Jesus said, "Your sins are forgiven" (Luke 5:20). They did not miss the implication that Jesus—the one who called himself the Son of man—was claiming for himself the power and authority of God. With their own eyes they saw the effects of sin being undone, but their hearts remained closed to Christ.

Jesus still has the authority and the power to forgive sin, take away guilt, and free us from the consequences of sin. The sacrament of Reconciliation makes the kingdom of God present to us as Jesus exercises his divine authority through the ministry of the priest to forgive us of our sin. Let us take advantage of this sacrament of forgiveness and take comfort from the truth that our sins are forgiven.

Luke 5:27-32

27 After this he went out, and saw a tax collector, named Levi,
sitting at the tax office; and he said to him, "Follow me." 28 And
he left everything, and rose and followed him.
29 And Levi made him a great feast in his house; and there was
a large company of tax collectors and others sitting at table with
them. 30 And the Pharisees and their scribes murmured against
his disciples, saying, "Why do you eat and drink with tax collectors
and sinners?" 31 And Jesus answered them, "Those who are well
have no need of a physician, but those who are sick; 32 I have not
come to call the righteous, but sinners to repentance."

When Jesus calls us to follow him, he wants to bring us life. Levi was a collaborator who worked for the Roman forces that subjugated his fellow Jews. He helped to carry out one of the most common methods of oppression and made his own living by taking a cut of the money he collected.

Jesus called Levi with the words, "Follow me" (Luke 5:27), and Levi left everything and followed the Lord. This man, better known as Matthew, was later chosen to be one of the Twelve, and eventually went on—according to tradition among the early Christians—to write the gospel that bears his name. Matthew's conversion was a great dramatic work of Jesus. A materialistic and reviled opportunist was transformed into one of the great exponents of the gospel of Christ.

Jesus invites us, as he did Matthew, to follow him. Who needs to respond? We all do. Jesus' words are a personal challenge to us. He came to bring all sinners to repentance because everybody sins and needs to repent (see Romans 3:23). Jesus Christ is the only righteous one. We may go to church. We may even try to pray, and that is good. But decent social behavior and high moral standards do not change our fallen condition and our need to follow Christ.

Before we can respond to Jesus' invitation, we must know we need him. Let us remember his words: "Those who are well have no need of a physician, but those who are sick; I have not come to call the righteous, but sinners to repentance" (Luke 5:31-32). We must all know that Jesus' call is a personal invitation to us. Let us accept his call and follow him.

"Lord Jesus, I want to receive the life you offer. Through the work of the Holy Spirit, help me to respond to the invitation you extend so that I can know the life of your kingdom every day. I want to follow you. Help me to answer your call."

Luke 5:33-39

33 And they said to him, "The disciples of John fast often and
offer prayers, and so do the disciples of the Pharisees, but yours eat
and drink." 34 And Jesus said to them, "Can you make wedding
guests fast while the bridegroom is with them? 35 The days will
come, when the bridegroom is taken away from them, and then
they will fast in those days." 36 He told them a parable also: "No

one tears a piece from a new garment and puts it upon an old garment; if he does, he will tear the new, and the piece from the new will not match the old. [37] And no one puts new wine into old wineskins; if he does, the new wine will burst the skins and it will be spilled, and the skins will be destroyed. [38] But new wine must be put into fresh wineskins. [39] And no one after drinking old wine desires new; for he says, 'The old is good.' "

It is often difficult for us to grasp the simple, life-changing message of Jesus. It was no less difficult for the people of Jesus' time to understand the same message, for their minds and thoughts were also bound by the conventions and ways of their day.

Jesus' teaching on fasting as well as the parable of the cloth and wineskins together addressed the problem facing the people: How were they to understand the kingdom of God with old minds formed by the world? The Pharisees asked Jesus questions about fasting and compared the fasting done by their disciples and those of John with the fasting done by Jesus' followers. Jesus tried to open their minds and help them understand that he was the one for whom they were fasting. He was the bridegroom for whom they were waiting and who was still with them.

Our Lord used parables and images drawn from daily life, in this case cloth and wineskins, to highlight his message and to encourage people to use their minds in new ways. Despite his teaching, many continued to try to understand the kingdom of God with minds formed by the ways and the teachings of the world; they tried to put "new wine into old wineskins" (Luke 5:37).

The same problem faces us today. We too try to put our old lives first and accept only those parts of Christian teaching which suit our particular situations. We need to pour the new wine of Jesus' life into new minds transformed by the Holy Spirit. Many of us struggle to understand the teachings of Christ and how they apply to our lives. We find it hard to use our minds in ways other than how we have always used them. Following Jesus, however, means new life, not new explanations to justify old ways of life.

"Lord Jesus, cleanse my mind of old ways of thinking and thoughts that prevent me from understanding your life-changing message. Send your Spirit to teach me about the kingdom of your Father. Free my mind from bondage to the conventions and ways of this day. Renew my mind so that I can understand and accept the teachings you reveal to us."

Luke 6:1-11

1 On a sabbath, while he was going through the grainfields, his
disciples plucked and ate some ears of grain, rubbing them in
their hands. 2 But some of the Pharisees said, "Why are you doing
what is not lawful to do on the sabbath?" 3 And Jesus answered,
"Have you not read what David did when he was hungry, he and
those who were with him: 4 how he entered the house of God,
and took and ate the bread of the Presence, which it is not lawful
for any but the priests to eat, and also gave it to those with him?"
5 And he said to them, "The Son of man is lord of the sabbath."
6 On another sabbath, when he entered the synagogue and
taught, a man was there whose right hand was withered. 7 And
the scribes and the Pharisees watched him, to see whether he
would heal on the sabbath, so that they might find an accusation
against him. 8 But he knew their thoughts, and he said to the
man who had the withered hand, "Come and stand here." And
he rose and stood there. 9 And Jesus said to them, "I ask you, is
it lawful on the sabbath to do good or to do harm, to save life or
to destroy it?" 10 And he looked around on them all, and said to

him, "Stretch out your hand." And he did so, and his hand was restored. [11] But they were filled with fury and discussed with one another what they might do to Jesus.

Because he wrote for a primarily Greek audience—who had little or no understanding of Jewish tradition—Luke frequently emphasized Jesus' confrontations with the Pharisees. So, when the Pharisees accused Jesus' disciples of breaking the sabbath, Jesus quickly defended them and pointed out that their actions were well within the boundaries of the law. Here, and in other instances, Jesus showed he had come not to abolish the law, but rather to fulfill it.

Jesus could see how the Pharisees sought to exercise control over God, establishing strict regulations and guidelines that often surpassed the requirements of the law. Their interpretation of the law concerning the sabbath, for example, focused on what should not be done on the day of rest. On the other hand, Jesus wanted to identify the heart of the law and invite his people to experience the freedom that was possible if they understood the central purpose of every one of God's laws. God had established the sabbath out of love, to give his people freedom from daily burdens so that they could come into his presence and worship him. To focus on what ought not to be done was to miss out on his invitation to rest and be refreshed.

As they walked through the grain fields, the disciples had the chance to enjoy Jesus' company. The throngs of people that often surrounded them were not around. This was an opportunity for the disciples to draw close to Jesus. They could pray with him and experience how close he was to the Father. This sabbath time of rest and quiet was an important part of their relationship with Jesus. Being refreshed with him in this way would enable them to bear the demands of the ministry Jesus wanted to entrust to them.

Even today, God wants the sabbath to be a time when we experience his saving freedom and joy. Like the Pharisees, we can cease working in order to satisfy the letter of the law, or we can quiet our hearts and rest in Jesus' presence. As we prepare for the sabbath, let us ask Jesus to reveal his heart of love and refresh us in preparation for the week ahead.

"Father, thank you for providing a day each week that we can spend with you. Thank you for sending the Holy Spirit, who enables us to draw close to you today."

Luke 6:12-19

12 In these days he went out into the hills to pray; and all night
he continued in prayer to God. 13 And when it was day, he called
his disciples, and chose from them twelve, whom he named
apostles; 14 Simon, whom he named Peter, and Andrew his
brother, and James and John, and Philip, and Bartholomew, 15 and
Matthew, and Thomas, and James the son of Alphaeus, and Simon
who was called the Zealot, 16 and Judas the son of James, and
Judas Iscariot, who became a traitor. 17 And he came down with
them and stood on a level place, with a great crowd of his disciples
and a great multitude of people from all Judea and Jerusalem and
the seacoast of Tyre and Sidon, who came to hear him and to be
healed of their diseases; 18 and those who were troubled with
unclean spirits were cured. 19 And all the crowd sought to touch
him, for power came forth from him and healed them all.

He went out into the hills to pray; and he spent the night in prayer to God. (Luke 6:12)

Prayer to his heavenly Father was the starting point for everything that Jesus said and did while on this earth. This prayer was not only a time for moments of special intimacy with his Father; it was always concerned with the fulfillment of the mission entrusted to him: "My food is to do the will of him who sent me and to accomplish his work" (John 4:34).

From among the disciples who followed him, Jesus was about to choose twelve as the foundation of his church. These twelve, later to be known as apostles, he called to a closer degree of intimacy with himself. He would instruct them about the Father and his loving plan, on how to live as he lived (in obedience to the Father), and do the works he performed (Luke 6:29-30). After his death and resurrection, these men would be responsible for carrying his mission of salvation to the whole world (see Matthew 28:19).

The night Jesus spent in prayer on this occasion (Luke 6:12) must have been one of intensity as he strove to choose the twelve. He saw what was in the heart of each one (see Acts 1:24). Despite his awareness of the impetuosity of Peter, the nationalism of Simon the Zealot, and the ambition of James and John, Jesus through prayer, could recognize in his choice of them the fulfillment of the Father's plan.

St. John Chrysostom spoke of prayer "as a supreme good… a partnership and union with God . . . a longing for God… a gift not given by man but out of God's grace." He said, "Our spirit should be quick to reach out toward God . . . when it is carrying out out its duties, caring for the needy, performing works of charity, giving generously in the service of others. . . Throughout the whole of our lives we may enjoy the benefit that comes from prayer if we devote a great deal of time to it" (*Homily: Prayer in the Light of the Spirit*).

If Jesus, who is Lord and Messiah (Luke 2:11) prays, what better recommendation can we have for the importance of prayer in our own lives? Let us learn an important lesson from him.

Luke 6:20-26

20 And he lifted up his eyes on his disciples, and said: "Blessed
are you poor, for yours is the kingdom of God. 21 Blessed are you
that hunger now, for you shall be satisfied. Blessed are you that
weep now, for you shall laugh.
22 "Blessed are you when men hate you, and when they exclude
you and revile you, and cast out your name as evil, on account of
the Son of man! 23 Rejoice in that day, and leap for joy, for
behold, your reward is great in heaven; for so their fathers did to
the prophets.
24 "But woe to you that are rich, for you have received your
consolation. 25 Woe to you that are full now, for you shall
hunger. Woe to you that laugh now, for you shall mourn and
weep. 26 Woe to you, when all men speak well of you, for so
their fathers did to the false prophets."

Whenever we read Jesus' teaching, it is helpful to keep one truth in mind: Jesus never spoke out of vague theory. He always spoke from his own experience of living in God's presence and seeking to please God. Consequently, when Jesus said that the poor, the hungry, the sorrowful, and the persecuted were blessed, he was not just presenting a theoretical agenda for the redistribution of wealth. He was speaking about the life of those who lived in, and were aware of, God's presence and whose entire lives were shaped by interaction and communion with God.

Jesus knew by experience what it meant to be poor and yet have the kingdom of God as his inheritance. The Son of Man, who had nowhere to lay his head (Luke 9:58), chose a life of simplicity because his heart was set on higher riches and goals (see Matthew 6:33). Praying throughout the night (Luke 6:12), fasting for forty days and forty nights (see Matthew 4:2), he subjected himself to hunger so that he could spend time with God in prayer, seeking his will and receiving his love.

Jesus mourned his disciples' unbelief (see Mark 9:19) and Jerusalem's rejection of his love (see Matthew 23:37), so full was his heart with a desire to give them everything the Father had given him (see John 16:14). Finally, he knew what it was to be hated, excluded and reviled as the Son of Man. He knew, like the prophets, that he would be persecuted and despised because his words struck against the hardness of sin in the human heart. But, again like the prophets, he could not keep from speaking out, so greatly did God's love for his people compel him.

The life that Jesus manifested is the same life he offers to us. On the surface these "blessings" may seem too costly or unappealing, but a deeper look can reveal the real treasure held out to us in Christ. The mourning, persecution, and hunger Jesus described are given us in proportion to our perception of the love and mercy of God. God will ask of us only what we're ready to give him willingly in love and gratitude. Let us commit ourselves to the great promise Jesus gave us: "Fear not, little flock, for it is your Father's good pleasure to give you the kingdom" (Luke 12:32).

Luke 6:27-35

27 "But I say to you that hear, Love your enemies, do good to
those who hate you, 28 bless those who curse you, pray for those
who abuse you. 29 To him who strikes you on the cheek, offer
the other also; and from him who takes away your cloak do not
withhold your coat as well. 30 Give to every one who begs from
you; and of him who takes away your goods do not ask them again.
31 And as you wish that men would do to you, do so to them.

32 "If you love those who love you, what credit is that to you?
For even sinners love those who love them. 33 And if you do
good to those who do good to you, what credit is that to you? For
even sinners do the same. 34 And if you lend to those from whom
you hope to receive, what credit is that to you? Even sinners lend
to sinners, to receive as much again. 35 But love your enemies,
and do good, and lend, expecting nothing in return; and your
reward will be great, and you will be sons of the Most High; for
he is kind to the ungrateful and the selfish."

Jesus' followers knew the tension of living in occupied territory. The soldiers and tax collectors of Herod Antipas, Rome's ruler, were ever-present reminders of their oppression. Consequently, when Jesus spoke to people about loving their enemies, he knew it would sound absurd to them. To love those who exploited them went against every natural inclination.

Indeed, Jesus was calling his followers to be supernatural, to be "sons of the Most High [who is] kind to the ungrateful and the selfish" (Luke 6:35). He was calling them to share in the love that originates in the heart of the Father. This love does not spring from admiration of the one who is loved. The enemy may not be admirable, after all. Neither does it mean approving the enemy's abuses. God's love extends to those who do not behave admirably, even to those who are sinning in the worst way—*at the very time they are sinning*. Neither is this love merely the absence of malice, but a compassionate desire for the other person's good.

To love in this way requires that we put aside our natural responses and open our hearts to divine love. It calls for humility and an emptying of ourselves to become like Jesus. He experienced the love that flowed from the Father toward him, and he made way for this grace from God to flow out through him to all people. When he was mistreated at his trial, he responded with true meekness (see John 18:19-24). He endured the insults with dignity and appealed to his offender with the truth and in love. Far from mere sentiment, this constructive kind of humility is active. It serves God through seeking the good of others. Jesus calls us to "love our enemies, and do good, and lend, expecting nothing in return" (Luke 6:35).

Although most of us do not live in enemy-occupied territory, we can nonetheless find ourselves at odds with co-workers, neighbors, even family members. As we rely on Jesus, he will supply us with charity. His grace will enable us to do good to others without concern for ourselves.

"Father, we praise you for sharing your perfect love with us through Christ. We thank you for every opportunity to practice humility. May our obedience glorify you!"

Luke 6:36-38

36 "Be merciful, even as your Father is merciful.
37 "Judge not, and you will not be judged; condemn not, and
you will not be condemned; forgive, and you will be forgiven;
38 give, and it will be given to you; good measure, pressed down,
shaken together, running over, will be put into your lap. For the
measure you give will be the measure you get back."

"Be merciful, even as your Father is merciful." (*Luke* 6:36)

This exhortation is the climax of Jesus' "Sermon on the Plain" in Luke's Gospel. In the Old Testament, mercy consisted of a combination of compassion and faithfulness. One who showed mercy was able to identify with the needs of others and to work to alleviate suffering. For the Israelites, the model of mercy was Yahweh himself (see Psalm 136). Not only did he rescue his people from bondage in Egypt, but he shielded them through their wanderings in the desert, and made of them a great nation. In every instance, Yahweh did not abandon his people but faithfully taught them and loved them.

We too are called to take on God's mercy as our own, to move and think as God does and thus be instruments of his peace and salvation in the world. Jesus assures us that if we imitate the Father, we will receive reward beyond measure. We will escape condemnation; we will know forgiveness; we will receive God's abundant generosity in our lives (Luke 6:37-38).

The question then arises: How can we hope to imitate God's boundless mercy? Is this asking too much? This is precisely why Jesus came to earth, "full of grace and truth" (John 1:14). Through Jesus, the beloved Son, we can become like the Father. Immediately after he told his disciples to imitate his Father's mercy, Jesus said, "Every one when he is fully taught will be like his teacher" (Luke 6:40). Jesus is our teacher, and we are called to become like him.

A disciple is one who endeavors to be like the master, taking on the master's character. As we attempt to understand and obey Jesus' words, as we look to him in prayer, as we walk in his way, he will transform our hearts and minds. As we seek to follow Jesus, God will give us the grace to do so. We will act not on our own power, but on the grace God gives us. By this free gift from God will we become like Jesus, to the point of showing divine mercy—compassion and faithfulness—to everyone we meet.

"Jesus, you are our master and teacher. By your Spirit, form us and change our hearts so that we can become increasingly like you. Help us to follow you, walking in the way you showed us. Jesus, we want to be merciful as you and your Father are merciful."

Luke 6:39-42

39 He also told them a parable: "Can a blind man lead a blind
man? Will they not both fall into a pit? 40 A disciple is not
above his teacher, but every one when he is fully taught will be
like his teacher. 41 Why do you see the speck that is in your
brother's eye, but do not notice the log that is in your own eye?
42 Or how can you say to your brother, 'Brother, let me take out
the speck that is in your eye,' when you yourself do not see the
log that is in your own eye? You hypocrite, first take the log out
of your own eye, and then you will see clearly to take out the
speck that is in your brother's eye."

Nothing delights the Father more than seeing his children care for one another in love and humility. Why? Because it is in our selfless service of our brothers and sisters that we most imitate his Son Jesus. Imagine, then, how it must break his heart when he sees different members of his family "serving" others with impure motives. Perhaps we consider ourselves as more advanced in the spiritual life than someone else. Or maybe we write off a neighbor as hopeless because he or she doesn't think the way we do. How quickly judgments form in our hearts—and we may be so accustomed to them that we do not even realize what we're doing.

It is this unawareness of pride that Jesus warned against when he told his followers to remove the "log" that was in their eyes before they tried to tend to the "speck" in their neighbor's (Luke 6:41-42). As Jesus said, such an attempt is like the blind trying to lead the blind: Neither one benefits!

So, what do we do? Should we stop trying to help others until we are completely holy? No one would ever help another soul. Of course we should continue to serve everyone we feel God puts in our path. But at the same time, we should be ever willing to have the Lord examine our hearts and bring us deeper repentance and healing. With the psalmist, we can pray: "Search me, O God, and know my heart! Try me and know my thoughts! And see if there be any wicked way in me" (Psalm 139:23-24).

Whenever you find yourself in a position of ministry—at home, in your parish, or at work—fix your eyes on Jesus. As a suffering servant, he embraced all the pain and weakness of God's people even to the point of death on a cross. So selfless was his love that his last breath was not an appeal for our punishment but a prayer for our forgiveness. Jesus swallowed up the darkness of self-love with the light of his self-giving, and by his Spirit, he can empower us to do the same.

"How much you love us, Jesus! You came to redeem us, not to judge us. Help us to become humble servants, as you were a humble servant. Teach us to be witnesses to the selfless love which you showed to us."

Luke 6:43-49

43 "For no good tree bears bad fruit, nor again does a bad tree
bear good fruit; 44 for each tree is known by its own fruit. For figs
are not gathered from thorns, nor are grapes picked from a bramble
bush. 45 The good man out of the good treasure of his heart

produces good, and the evil man out of his evil treasure produces
evil; for out of the abundance of the heart his mouth speaks.
46 "Why do you call me 'Lord, Lord,' and not do what I tell you?
47 Every one who comes to me and hears my words and does
them, I will show you what he is like: 48 he is like a man building
a house, who dug deep, and laid the foundation upon rock; and
when a flood arose, the stream broke against that house, and could
not shake it, because it had been well built. 49 But he who hears
and does not do them is like a man who built a house on the
ground without a foundation; against which the stream broke, and
immediately it fell, and the ruin of that house was great."

What makes a tree strong? Doesn't it have to do with the condition of its root system? If it's rooted in good soil, and is receiving enough light and water, it will be a strong, healthy tree and bear good fruit. But if the soil is poor and it doesn't receive the necessary amounts of light and water, the roots become unhealthy and can no longer support the tree. Its fruit—if any—will be poor as well.

Jesus used this illustration to teach a very fundamental lesson: Unless we remain rooted in him, the "true vine" (John 15:1), we will not produce fruit that is pleasing to the Father. On the other hand, if we do stay close to him, we will become more and more like him and the fruit we bear will be continuously more Christ-like.

Have you ever tried to imitate someone you admired? You probably started out well, but gave up once you realized how hard it is to be someone you're not. The good news is that with Jesus, it's a different story. He died and rose so that we can be like him, so that our efforts would bring remarkable results. We can bear the same fruit that he bears because we're baptized into his life; we're from the same tree. He has given us his Spirit to transform us more and more into his image and likeness. As we stay close to him in prayer and remain obedient to his commands, we will find ourselves changing at the very root of our being—our hearts—so that the whole tree will be pleasing to our Father.

In Luke 6:46-49, Jesus makes the same point using the image of a well-founded house. The foundation on which we build must be solid. Jesus is the only firm foundation there is. If we try to build on anything else—even our own efforts—to please God, our house will not be able to bear the weight of life in this world. With Jesus as our foundation, nothing that comes against us will prevail.

"Lord, come and transform us more fully into your image. Root us into your life so that we can be holy and pleasing to your Father."

A Devotional Commentary on Luke

Jesus' Power, Compassion, and Wisdom

Luke
7:1–9:50

Luke 7:1-10

1 After he had ended all his sayings in the hearing of the
people he entered Caperna-um. 2 Now a centurion had a slave
who was dear to him, who was sick and at the point of death.
3 When he heard of Jesus, he sent to him elders of the Jews,
asking him to come and heal his slave. 4 And when they came
to Jesus, they besought him earnestly, saying, "He is worthy to
have you do this for him, 5 for he loves our nation, and he built
us our synagogue." 6 And Jesus went with them. When he was
not far from the house, the centurion sent friends to him, saying
to him, "Lord, do not trouble yourself, for I am not worthy to
have you come under my roof; 7 therefore I did not presume to
come to you. But say the word, and let my servant be healed.
8 For I am a man set under authority, with soldiers under me: and
I say to one, 'Go,' and he goes; and to another, 'Come,' and he
comes; and to my slave, 'Do this,' and he does it." 9 When Jesus
heard this he marveled at him, and turned and said to the
multitude that followed him, "I tell you, not even in Israel have I
found such faith." 10 And when those who had been sent
returned to the house, they found the slave well.

The centurion in Luke was a man of solid faith, reflecting a confidence in Jesus which was total and absolute. His attitude and behavior silently acknowledged Jesus' authority over all aspects of human life. Confronted with the dire illness of a beloved servant, the centurion turned with calm assurance to Jesus. He did not become preoccupied with difficulties, upset by circumstances, or dominated by his emotions. Instead, he sought out the authority which rests in Jesus' word as the clear solution to his personal problem.

The first letter of Peter lauds the faith of those who came to accept and trust in Jesus after his death and resurrection. "Without having seen him you love him; though you do not now see him you believe in him and rejoice with unutterable and exalted joy. As the outcome of your faith you obtain the salvation of your souls" (1 Peter 1:8-9). We can see how well these words describe the faith of the centurion.

The centurion did not feel it necessary to make his appeal to Jesus in person, but sent two sets of emissaries instead; first two Jewish elders and then some of his friends (Luke 7:3,6). To him, Jesus was clearly a man upon whom the favor of the Lord rested, a man whose authority extended beyond the mortal sphere. In view of this, and in true humility, the centurion considered himself unworthy to have Jesus enter his house. So highly did he esteem the power of Jesus that he required only a word to accomplish the favor he was seeking. "Say the word, and let my servant be healed" (7:7). The servant was healed—through the power of Jesus and the faith of the centurion.

This incident can help to strengthen us in our times of need, when circumstances cause us distress and we are made aware of our own inadequacies. Jesus' authority has not been eroded by the years. His promise is as valid now as it was 2,000 years ago: "If you abide in me, and my words abide in you, ask whatever you will, and it shall be done for you" (John 15.7). Pray today that the Lord will increase your faith, especially during times of tension and doubt, so that you may confidently call upon his word as the true source of your strength.

Luke 7:11-17

11 Soon afterward he went to a city called Nain, and his
disciples and a great crowd went with him. 12 As he drew near to
the gate of the city, behold, a man who had died was being
carried out, the only son of his mother, and she was a widow; and
a large crowd from the city was with her. 13 And when the Lord
saw her, he had compassion on her and said to her, "Do not
weep." 14 And he came and touched the bier, and the bearers
stood still. And he said, "Young man, I say to you, arise." 15 And
the dead man sat up, and began to speak. And he gave him to his
mother. 16 Fear seized them all; and they glorified God, saying,
"A great prophet has arisen among us!" and "God has visited his
people!" 17 And this report concerning him spread through the
whole of Judea and all the surrounding country.

What would have drawn Jesus to a funeral march for an only son of a widow? Was it curiosity? Was he attracted by the commotion and crying, the ritual mourning that was part of Middle Eastern funerals? Above all other factors, Jesus was drawn to this scene because of the compassion that always attracts him to the sorrowful and needy.

When he came upon a leper, he reached out and healed him because he was "moved with pity" (Mark 1:41). When the disciples tried to keep children away from him, his tenderness moved him to welcome them back (Luke 18:15-16). Similarly, in this scene, it was Jesus' compassion for the widow that drew him to her side: "When the Lord saw her, he had compassion on her and said to her, 'Do not weep' " (7:13).

We too were once spiritually dead with no hope. But Jesus had compassion on us and, through his death on the cross, he raised us from eternal death to new life in him. Just as the people of Nain praised God when they witnessed a wonderful miracle in their midst, so we can rejoice and praise God for the great work he is doing in our lives. In his mercy, God chose to rescue us and draw us to himself, revealing his love to us so that we would embrace his salvation: "We love, because he first loved us" (1 John 4:19).

Take some time in prayer today to write down the different ways you have experienced Jesus' compassion and tenderness. Think about the way he rescued you from death through his cross and gave you new life in the Spirit. Try to recall specific situations when you knew his comfort, wisdom, or strength. Look at different members of your family and consider how God has cared for them. As recipients of such love and grace, we are now called to share that love with those around us. Let us ask the Spirit to teach us to love as Jesus loves so that we can become ambassadors of Christ in this world.

"Lord, may your compassion for us fill us with compassion for others, especially those in our families and those who have no knowledge of your great love and mercy."

Luke 7:18-23

18 The disciples of John told him of all these things. 19 And
John, calling to him two of his disciples, sent them to the Lord,
saying, "Are you he who is to come, or shall we look for
another?' " 20 And when the men had come to him, they said,
"John the Baptist has sent us to you, saying, 'Are you he who is
to come, or shall we look for another?' " 21 In that hour he cured
many of diseases and plagues and evil spirits, and on many that
were blind he bestowed sight. 22 And he answered them, "Go
and tell John what you have seen and heard: the blind receive

their sight, the lame walk, lepers are cleansed, and the deaf hear, the dead are raised up, the poor have good news preached to them. [23] And blessed is he who takes no offense at me."

Are you he who is to come, or shall we look for another (Luke 7:19)

Jesus didn't give a "yes" or "no" answer to John's disciples. As he said elsewhere, "If I bear witness to myself, my testimony is not true; there is another who bears witness to me" (John 5:31-32). So he gave them a scriptural answer that was far more revealing. The prophet had described the joy of the redeemed: "Then the eyes of the blind shall be opened, and the cars of the deaf unstopped" (Isaiah 35:5). He had also written of the year of the Lord's favor (61:1-2), the passage Jesus quoted in the synagogue at Nazareth (Luke 4:18-19).

The healings Jesus had performed, the good news he preached, all reflected the work of the Messiah in the prophetic literature. This would be a far more meaningful answer to John the Baptist than a simple "yes" or "no." John's disciples were to report back to him that Jesus' works were indeed the fulfillment of the prophecies spoken about the Messiah, "the one who is to come" (Luke 3:16). But Jesus added a further message: "Blessed is he who takes no offense at me" (7:23). Jesus' words were a challenge to John—as they are to all of us—to rid our minds of preconceived notions of how God should act and for whom.

In Jesus we are all blessed because in him we receive life. He came, healed, preached, suffered, died and rose again so that we might have a share in that infinite, uncreated life that he has possessed since before time began as the Word of God, the only Son of the Father. He came to reconcile us with the Father and to impart to us the power of the Holy Spirit. To all who find no stumbling block in him, but who believe and accept him, he grants full participation in the life of the Trinity. How blessed we are! How eagerly we should seek, believe in, and receive that life! Let us prayerfully examine the testimony of the scriptures, of the saints, of faithful people today, and believe what we see and hear.

"Lord Jesus, we acknowledge you as the one who has come so that we might have life, and have it to the fullest. Strengthen our faith that we might more fully live the life you have won for us."

Luke 7:24-30

24 When the messengers of John had gone, he began to speak
to the crowds concerning John: "What did you go out into the
wilderness to behold? A reed shaken by the wind? 25 What then
did you go out to see? A man clothed in soft raiment? Behold,
those who are gorgeously appareled and live in luxury are in
kings' courts. 26 What then did you go out to see? A prophet?
Yes, I tell you, and more than a prophet. 27 This is he of whom it
is written, 'Behold, I send my messenger before thy face, who
shall prepare thy way before thee.' 28 I tell you, among those
born of women none is greater than John; yet he who is least in
the kingdom of God is greater than he." 29 (When they heard
this all the people and the tax collectors justified God, having
been baptized with the baptism of John; 30 but the Pharisees and
the lawyers rejected the purpose of God for themselves, not
having been baptized by him.)

John the Baptist lived a simple, disciplined life in the wilderness. He wore camel's hair and a leather belt, ate locusts and wild honey (see Mark 1:6), and abstained from bread and wine (Luke 7:33). His lifestyle helped prevent him from being distracted by the things of the world. And so, he grew in his openness and desire for God.

John's desire and purity of heart opened him to God so that he could recognize Jesus as the Lamb of God, the promised Messiah. John himself did not recognize Jesus, but God revealed who Jesus was to him (see John 1:31). If John's mind had been closed to the Spirit of God, he would not have recognized Jesus and probably would have been envious of his ministry. But since John sought God single-mindedly (as reflected through his prayer and indifference to the attractions of the world), he found Jesus.

After hearing about the miracles, healings, and teachings of Jesus, John—who was then imprisoned by Herod—sent two of his disciples to ask Jesus if he was "the one who is to come" (Luke 7:18-19). In so doing, he was discerning the validity of Jesus' teaching and works which reflected compassion, love, and forgiveness, particularly in light of his own beliefs concerning the severity of the judgment that was to come (3:17). If John's mind had been closed to the Spirit's revealing word, he might have rejected Jesus as the Messiah, since he did not meet his expectations.

The people who had received the baptism of John praised God when they heard Jesus speak because their minds had been opened to God through the baptism John had administered (Luke 7:29). The Pharisees and lawyers, on the other hand, refused the baptism and closed themselves to God. Blinded to God's plan of salvation, they "rejected God's purpose for themselves" (7:30).

To find Jesus, we—like John—must seek to open our spirits, minds, and hearts to the Holy Spirit. Closing ourselves to the distractions around us and asking for the Spirit's enlightenment, we will grow in our ability to recognize God's work in Christ Jesus.

"Lord Jesus, my human mind alone cannot comprehend the

plan of God. Enlighten my mind with your Spirit so that I might find you, experience your steadfast love and forgiveness, and accept your will for my life."

Luke 7:31-35

31 "To what then shall I compare the men of this generation,
and what are they like? 32 They are like children sitting in the
market place and calling to one another, 'We piped to you, and
you did not dance; we wailed, and you did not weep.' 33 For John
the Baptist has come eating no bread and drinking no wine; and
you say, 'He has a demon.' 34 The Son of man has come eating
and drinking; and you say, 'Behold, a glutton and a drunkard, a
friend of tax collectors and sinners!' 35 Yet wisdom is justified by
all her children."

Wisdom is justified by all her children. (Luke 7:35)

How sad it is that there are some who cling to their own righteousness so tightly that they are closed to God's grace. Jesus came to deliver the good news of salvation to all men and women. The gospels are full of accounts of people who sought him out and placed their faith in him. None were disappointed. Yet Jesus did not confine himself to those who sought him. Earlier in this chapter, we read how Jesus came across a funeral for a young man. Of his own initiative, and moved with pity, he reached out to the corpse and brought the young man back to life.

All that is required to receive grace from God is that we listen to him. If we listen and believe, he accomplishes the rest. He will vindicate his grace by seeing that it bears fruit in us in keeping with its intention. We need only keep from obstructing its development. It is as if Jesus is a great track and field trainer. He recruits for his team anyone who will listen to his instruction and training. He doesn't expect athletic prowess in other sports, and he will even accept those lacking coordination. Under his tutelage, everyone makes progress. Those who listen closely succeed beyond their abilities because of the power of his grace.

We can take heart in knowing that Jesus seeks out everyone—even those ignored by the powerful and wealthy. Throughout this chapter, Luke shows Jesus reaching out to a pagan, a widow, a prostitute, handicapped persons, and the demon-possessed. Jesus never discriminated; he offered his healing and mercy to everyone.

Even today, God greatly desires to touch those around us. The hope of the gospel is for them. If we listen to the Spirit, he will show us how to share the good news with our friends, neighbors, and family members. And, he will pour out his grace to those who listen and believe—for his faithfulness is not dependent upon our righteousness, but upon his unconditional love.

"Thank you, Father, for giving us your Son. Because he is faithful to us, we need never despair of your love. Help us to trust in the power of your grace to flow through us to everyone around us."

Luke 7:36-50

36 One of the Pharisees asked him to eat with him, and he
went into the Pharisee's house, and sat at table. 37 And behold, a
woman of the city, who was a sinner, when she learned that he
was at table in the Pharisee's house, brought an alabaster flask of

ointment, [38] and standing behind him at his feet, weeping, she
began to wet his feet with her tears, and wiped them with the
hair of her head, and kissed his feet, and anointed them with the
ointment. [39] Now when the Pharisee who had invited him saw
it, he said to himself, "If this man were a prophet, he would have
known who and what sort of woman this is who is touching him,
for she is a sinner." [40] And Jesus answering said to him, "Simon,
I have something to say to you." And he answered, "What is it,
Teacher?" [41] "A certain creditor had two debtors; one owed five
hundred denarii, and the other fifty. [42] When they could not
pay, he forgave them both. Now which of them will love him
more?" [43] Simon answered, "The one, I suppose, to whom he
forgave more." And he said to him, "You have judged rightly."
[44] Then turning toward the woman he said to Simon, "Do you
see this woman? I entered your house, you gave me no water for
my feet, but she has wet my feet with her tears and wiped them
with her hair. [45] You gave me no kiss, but from the time I came
in she has not ceased to kiss my feet. [46] You did not anoint my
head with oil, but she has anointed my feet with ointment.
[47] Therefore I tell you, her sins, which are many, are forgiven, for
she loved much; but he who is forgiven little, loves little."
[48] And he said to her, "Your sins are forgiven." [49] Then those
who were at table with him began to say among themselves,
"Who is this, who even forgives sins?" [50] And he said to the
woman, "Your faith has saved you; go in peace."

Luke's Gospel is full of stories that contrast the rich and the poor, the proud and the humble. In Jesus' encounter with the sinful woman, the contrast is between this woman and a Pharisee whose prejudices blind him to Jesus' love. To be fair, we should credit this Pharisee with inviting Jesus to dinner and even calling Jesus, "Teacher." His actions showed some respect for Jesus. The woman, however, demonstrated what can happen when we experience Jesus not just as a teacher, but as a Savior filled with love and mercy.

Water for the feet, a kiss, and oil for the head were not gestures offered to every guest. They were reserved only for people deserving high respect and regard. What is remarkable is that the woman surpassed each of these expectations: She washed Jesus' feet with her tears, not ordinary water. She kissed, not his head, but his feet. And she anointed him with costly perfume, not everyday olive oil, as would have been expected. Such an outpouring of reverence showed how deeply this woman must have loved Jesus!

We might think that this woman's love pleased Jesus and so elicited his response of forgiveness. However, the original Greek text hints that her love was the result of her having received mercy and love from God first, not as a result of her actions. "Therefore I tell you, her sins, which are many, are forgiven, for she loved much" (Luke 7:47). The "for" in this sentence—*hoti* in Greek—is best understood to mean "for this reason." Her sins, which were many, were forgiven and for this reason she loved much.

What is even more remarkable is that this woman had not even seen the fullest manifestation of Jesus' love and mercy—the cross—yet she responded so freely. Without the physical evidence, she experienced Jesus' mercy, and her life was changed. Every stain of sin, all guilt and shame, all fear and sense of unworthiness, were wiped away, and she was filled with love and gratitude.

"Lord, what a merciful God you are. We love you because you have so perfectly loved us. We want to pour out our gratitude to you today, and every day, as we pray, share your word with our friends, and demonstrate your love through acts of kindness and reconciliation."

Luke 8:1-3

1 Soon afterward he went on through cities and villages,
preaching and bringing the good news of the kingdom of God.
And the twelve were with him, 2 and also some women who had
been healed of evil spirits and infirmities: Mary, called
Magdalene, from whom seven demons had gone out, 3 and
Joanna, the wife of Chuza, Herod's steward, and Susanna, and
many others, who provided for them out of their means.

When God moves, creation trembles, as if the greatness of God were bursting the narrow confines of human existence. Commonplace expectations tumble down, and things unexpected and unimagined are experienced: "My thoughts are not your thoughts, neither are your ways my ways, says the Lord" (Isaiah 55:8).

When Jesus became a man and dwelt among us, he expanded the boundaries of what people expected from the Messiah. He went about "preaching and bringing the good news of the kingdom of God" (Luke 8:1). The good news is startling: God intends salvation for everyone—not just the deserving, faithful, or religious, but for every man and woman ever in existence.

This was almost incomprehensible to the Jews, God's chosen people. That God should redeem the nations—even the immoral, unbelieving heathen—was unthinkable! In fact, however, it was—and still is—true. No one is excluded from God's love or his desire to share his life personally and intimately. No one on this earth is beyond the reach of God's love or too steeped in sin for his power to redeem.

The twelve apostles and the women who traveled with Jesus (Luke 8:2) were not what was expected of the Messiah king's retinue. Fishermen, tax collectors, women—poor, socially marginal, and unschooled in their religion—were a startling departure from Jewish convention, and testimony to the unimaginable wisdom and ways of God. But God's wisdom shatters the restrictions of our minds and, in Jesus, God reconciles men and women, Jews and Gentiles, rich and poor, healthy and sick, righteous and outcast, often in unimaginable ways.

In Jesus, the kingdom of God is opened once and for all to everyone: the lowly and marginal, the prominent and influential. There is a joy that comes with the broadening of our human boundaries: Delight and exultation in the love of God as it shines through the darkness of our limited expectations. The Holy Spirit who dwells in us will teach us the truth of Jesus. This truth—the realities and thoughts of Almighty God—is not something we can conjure up or know on our own. It is completely other than our thoughts; we need the Holy Spirit to guide us in all truth (see John 16:13). Let us turn to him daily for the wisdom and knowledge that come only from God.

"Jesus, shatter our preconceived ideas and biases so that we may think as you think, love as you love, and choose the ways and plans that you have ordained from before all time."

Luke 8:4-15

4 And when a great crowd came together and people from
town after town came to him, he said in a parable: 5 "A sower
went out to sow his seed; and as he sowed, some fell along the
path, and was trodden under foot, and the birds of the air
devoured it. 6 And some fell on the rock; and as it grew up, it
withered away, because it had no moisture. 7 And some fell
among thorns; and the thorns grew with it and choked it. 8 And

some fell into good soil and grew, and yielded a hundredfold." As
he said this, he called out, "He who has ears to hear, let him hear."
9 And when his disciples asked him what this parable meant,
10 he said, "To you it has been given to know the secrets of the
kingdom of God; but for others they are in parables, so that
seeing they may not see, and hearing they may not understand.
11 Now the parable is this: The seed is the word of God. 12 The
ones along the path are those who have heard; then the devil
comes and takes away the word from their hearts, that they may
not believe and be saved. 13 And the ones on the rock are those
who, when they hear the word, receive it with joy; but these
have no root, they believe for a while and in time of temptation
fall away. 14 And as for what fell among the thorns, they are
those who hear, but as they go on their way they are choked by
the cares and riches and pleasures of life, and their fruit does not
mature. 15 And as for that in the good soil, they are those who,
hearing the word, hold it fast in an honest and good heart, and
bring forth fruit with patience.

How exciting that God keeps offering us opportunity after opportunity to turn from the things that keep us from him and to receive his blessings! In the parable of the seed, Jesus taught his disciples to examine the way they live so that they could bear great fruit as they experience his life and love.

When we are baptized, God generously gives us the seed of his new life. But, because of the darkness in the world around us, and because of the drive toward sin within us, the growth of this seed is far from automatic. The Evil One is always looking for a way to steal God's word from us and so arrest our growth in Christ. We become distracted by the worries and riches and pleasures of life. In our hearts we experience fear and darkness.

These difficulties can discourage us and make us anxious. Yet Jesus taught this parable so that we might have hope. As we cast off our sinful desires and resist the sin in the world around us, the imperishable seed of new life can grow and produce fruit that is pleasing to God and to us. By tending the seed—that is, by yielding to God's work in us—we give the wonder of divine life a chance to displace our sinful tendencies.

How do we yield to God? Jesus asks us to pray, to spend time studying his word, to examine our lives in light of his teaching, and to serve others in love. When we obey him, we will experience his love for us. And this experience will transform us so that over time, we become more and more like him. Our love for the Lord and our obedience to him—as well as our love and forgiveness of others—will uproot our old life and give the new life room to grow. God only asks us to take a few steps in faith each day. He will bless even the smallest steps and give us a hunger for even more of him.

"How loving you are, Lord Jesus! You cared enough for us that you came and taught us how to live. Bless my steps today as I seek to cultivate the seed of your new life in me. Teach me to trust in your grace with every step I take."

Luke 8:16-18

16 "No one after lighting a lamp covers it with a vessel, or puts it
under a bed, but puts it on a stand, that those who enter may see
the light. 17 For nothing is hid that shall not be made manifest,
nor anything secret that shall not be known and come to light.
18 Take heed then how you hear; for to him who has will more be
given, and from him who has not, even what he thinks that he
has will be taken away."

To him who has will more be given. (Luke 8:18)

How perplexing Jesus' words can sometimes seem! At first glance, we may feel that he was critical of those who, through no fault of their own, were lacking. Yet, on deeper examination, we realize that he was talking about what had been already generously given to all his hearers: the word of his preaching. The distinction he made was in how this word was received. He commended those who received the word with gratitude and faith, because they would willingly apply it to their lives and bear fruit (Luke 8:15).

Encouraging his followers to pay close attention to his words, Jesus promised: "Nothing is hid that shall not be made manifest" (Luke 8:17). Every secret of the kingdom of God will eventually be revealed. Every mystery that we puzzle over—why Jesus had to die on the cross, why God allows suffering, why some members of our family are more open to God than others—will be uncovered, and we will see with a clarity far beyond the limitations of our human intellects.

How do we find the answers to these questions? We find it through prayerful meditation and study of God's word. The more time we spend immersing ourselves in the wisdom of God, the more our minds will be formed according to God's mind. We will learn to think the way God thinks, and we will know the peace that comes from pondering "the depth of the riches and wisdom and knowledge of God" (Romans 11:33). With St. Paul, we will be able to proclaim: "We have the mind of Christ" (1 Corinthians 2:16).

Jesus promised that if we hold fast to what we have received, it will grow and bear fruit in us. As we are nourished by God's word, the light of his wisdom will shine out from us, penetrating the darkness of the world. The witness of our lives will draw others to us, and we will be able to share with them the wisdom we have received from God. Let us allow God's word in scripture to form us so that we can become Jesus' ambassadors to the world.

"Blessed Jesus, thank you for the light you have placed inside us through your word. May your light within us shine out to all those we meet. Come, Lord, and conquer the darkness with the marvelous light of your truth."

Luke 8:19-21

[19] Then his mother and his brethren came to him, but they
could not reach him for the crowd. [20] And he was told, "Your
mother and your brethren are standing outside, desiring to see
you." [21] But he said to them, "My mother and my brethren are
those who hear the word of God and do it."

Luke observed that the gospel grew in ever-widening circles, emanating from Galilee out to the entire world. Everywhere Jesus preached the good news and transformed the lives of those who believed. Jesus frequently emphasized that his disciples had to hear and obey this gospel: "Take heed then how you hear" (Luke 8:18).

Luke juxtaposed one such exhortation with an appearance of Jesus' family, who wanted to see him. Jesus seized this opportunity to teach once more about true discipleship: "My mother and my brethren are those who hear the word of God and do it" (Luke 8:21). Perhaps Jesus' statement may have seemed odd, seemingly diminishing his family's significance. But Jesus knew he could point to his mother, Mary, as a supreme illustration of one who hears and accepts the word of God.

We may presume that Mary was devoted to God's word in the Hebrew scriptures; only there could she have learned to cherish God's promise of salvation. Consequently, Mary grew sensitive to recognizing the Lord's voice. Her practice of listening to God enabled her to reply readily to the angel of the Lord: "Let it be to me according to your word" (Luke 1:38). She truly was one who heard the word of God and did it.

By faith, Mary gave herself over freely and completely to God's will. Luke portrayed Mary as declaring: "My soul magnifies the Lord" (Luke 1:46). This is a powerful and humbling statement: It deflates self and places God superior to all else. In this way, Mary chose God's will above her own.

These qualities of hearing and obeying God's word make Mary the model of a true disciple of Jesus. By pointing to her example, Jesus taught what it means to come to him, for she was one who did pay attention to how she listened.

"Lord Jesus, help us to imitate your mother, a true disciple in the way she heard the word and kept it. Being your disciple does not depend on blood, birth, or sex, but on hearing and doing your will. Send me your Holy Spirit and help me to put off everything that deadens my ability to respond to you. Help me to live as your true disciple, and by so doing, bring your presence into the world."

Luke 8:22-25

22 One day he got into a boat with his disciples, and he said
to them, "Let us go across to the other side of the lake." So they
set out, 23 and as they sailed he fell asleep. And a storm of wind
came down on the lake, and they were filling with water, and
were in danger. 24 And they went and woke him, saying,
"Master, Master, we are perishing!" And he awoke and rebuked
the wind and the raging waves; and they ceased, and there was

a calm. [25] He said to them, "Where is your faith?" And they were afraid, and they marveled, saying to one another, "Who then is this, that he commands even wind and water, and they obey him?"

Many Christians today face problems similar to those of the apostles in the storm-tossed boat; like them, our lives are frequently run by our emotions, rather than by our faith. Before embarking, the disciples had been happy and excited to be with Jesus. They had seen him preach to large crowds; perform signs, wonders, and miracles in abundance; and respond generously to all who approached him. There was very little in these events to test their faith. Now, tossed by the savage wind and waves, they cried out, "We are perishing!" (Luke 8:24). They were overcome by fear.

Every day we run into situations that can throw us back on our emotions instead of on our faith. A critical remark from our spouse or employer, success or failure in an important project, or the healing or re-emergence of a long-standing medical problem all can send our emotions soaring or plummeting.

This little story can be helpful to recall in times of trial. Three companions—Faith, Fact, and Feeling—were walking together, one behind the other, along the top of a wall. Feeling, who was last (and who had notoriously poor balance), suddenly stumbled and fell from the wall. He lay groaning on the ground. Faith, distracted by the loss of his companion, also slipped and fell from the wall. Only Fact remained. He was not easily upset and stood firm as a rock. By doing so, he was able to help Faith get back up. At last, between them, Feeling was restored and rejoined them on their journey.

The moral of the story: Despite what our feelings or emotions may tell us, the facts remain the same. We must daily use our intelligence to recall what God has done for us through his Son, Jesus

Christ. We can proclaim to ourselves: "I know Jesus died for my sins; I know God loves me; I know his Spirit dwells within me as his temple." As we use our minds to reaffirm the truths of our faith, we will experience confident fellowship with God rather than the emotional ups and downs to which we are so often subjected.

Luke 8:26-39

26 Then they arrived at the country of the Gerasenes, which is
opposite Galilee. 27 And as he stepped out on land, there met
him a man from the city who had demons; for a long time he
had worn no clothes, and he lived not in a house but among the
tombs.
28 When he saw Jesus, he cried out and fell down before him,
and said with a loud voice, "What have you to do with me, Jesus,
Son of the Most High God? I beseech you, do not torment me."
29 For he had commanded the unclean spirit to come out of the
man. (For many a time it had seized him; he was kept under
guard, and bound with chains and fetters, but he broke the bonds
and was driven by the demon into the desert.) 30 Jesus then
asked him, "What is your name?" And he said, "Legion"; for
many demons had entered him. 31 And they begged him not to
command them to depart into the abyss. 32 Now a large herd of
swine was feeding there on the hillside; and they begged him to
let them enter these. So he gave them leave. 33 Then the
demons came out of the man and entered the swine, and the
herd rushed down the steep bank into the lake and were
drowned.
34 When the herdsmen saw what had happened, they fled, and
told it in the city and in the country. 35 Then people went out to

see what had happened, and they came to Jesus, and found the man from whom the demons had gone, sitting at the feet of Jesus, clothed and in his right mind; and they were afraid. [36] And those who had seen it told them how he who had been possessed with demons was healed. [37] Then all the people of the surrounding country of the Gerasenes asked him to depart from them; for they were seized with great fear; so he got into the boat and returned.
[38] The man from whom the demons had gone begged that he might be with him; but he sent him away, saying, [39] "Return to your home, and declare how much God has done for you." And he went away, proclaiming throughout the whole city how much Jesus had done for him.

Jesus had just sailed across the Sea of Galilee to Gadara when he encountered this possessed man. Day and night, the demoniac would storm and rage in a violent frenzy, and no one could subdue him. Any passer-by was at risk. Yet, *one* command from Jesus caused the demons to leave their human victim and plunge to their own destruction.

The word "demoniac" may not mean much to us anymore. We may have to stop and consider what was actually occurring with this demon-possessed man. He was utterly helpless to change his state. The evil within him not only had its way with him, it *owned* him. He was so controlled by evil that he not only terrorized others, but also abused himself (see Mark 5:5). He was without hope—abandoned to the despair that fueled his savagery. No one even dared to walk past this man.

Yet, in the face of such evil, Jesus simply walked up and gave *one command* to turn the whole situation around. Like everything else in creation, even these demons were subject to Jesus. The One through whom and for whom all was created has authority over every element—in heaven, on earth, and even under the earth. It is important that we know this, because the evil that possessed this man is the same evil that besieges our world today. Nothing has changed. And, neither has Jesus' power and authority.

Jesus wants to bind evil and bring his light into our lives. We must never be afraid to go to him for healing and deliverance. He will expose all darkness and bring the radiance of his love to all who seek him. Let us listen to him as he speaks to us in prayer and through the scriptures. He wants to live within us. Whatever problems or evil we may face, we can be sure that Jesus is in control. We can count on him to help us face even our darkest hour.

"Lord Jesus, your power is limitless. In our darkest hour, all we need is one word from you. We place before you our needs and the needs of our loved ones. Lift the darkness from our lives. Fill us with the radiance of your love."

Luke 8:40-56

40 Now when Jesus returned, the crowd welcomed him, for they
were all waiting for him. 41 And there came a man named Jairus,
who was a ruler of the synagogue; and falling at Jesus' feet he
besought him to come to his house, 42 for he had an only
daughter, about twelve years of age, and she was dying.
As he went, the people pressed round him. 43 And a woman
who had had a flow of blood for twelve years and had spent all her
living upon physicians and could not be healed by anyone,
44 came up behind him, and touched the fringe of his garment;
and immediately her flow of blood ceased. 45 And Jesus said,
"Who was it that touched me?" When all denied it, Peter said,
"Master, the multitudes surround you and press upon you!" 46

But Jesus said, "Some one touched me; for I perceive that power
has gone forth from me." 47 And when the woman saw that she
was not hidden, she came trembling, and falling down before
him declared in the presence of all the people why she had
touched him, and how she had been immediately healed. 48 And
he said to her, "Daughter, your faith has made you well; go in
peace."
49 While he was still speaking, a man from the ruler's house
came and said, "Your daughter is dead; do not trouble the Teacher
any more." 50 But Jesus on hearing this answered him, "Do not
fear; only believe, and she shall be well." 51 And when he came
to the house, he permitted no one to enter with him, except
Peter and John and James, and the father and mother of the
child. 52 And all were weeping and bewailing her; but he said,
"Do not weep; for she is not dead but sleeping." 53 And they
laughed at him, knowing that she was dead. 54 But taking her by
the hand he called, saying, "Child, arise." 55 And her spirit
returned, and she got up at once; and he directed that something
should be given her to eat. 56 And her parents were amazed; but
he charged them to tell no one what had happened.

Do you ever find yourself thinking that miracles don't really happen today? Luke recounted two powerful miracles that occurred in the lives of very ordinary people who sought Jesus out. One of these miracles was Jesus' raising an official's daughter from the dead, and the other was his healing a hemorrhaging woman who believed that if she touched Jesus' cloak, she would be made well. As these believers stepped out in faith, they experienced God's healing power in remarkable ways.

Describing the woman's healing, Luke used the Greek word *sozo*, which can mean both "to heal" and "to save" or "to deliver."

By choosing such a word, Luke wanted to point his readers beyond the physical aspect of this miracle to show the deeper work that had taken place. Not only did Jesus heal this woman of the effects of sin, he also healed her of sin itself, bringing her into a deeper relationship with God. She who was once considered an outcast and unclean was welcomed by Jesus and restored to her original dignity.

Jesus Christ is the Savior of the world, "the same yesterday and today and for ever" (Hebrews 13:8). He never changes in his desire to heal us, both physically and spiritually. Jesus wants to save us from sin on a daily basis so that we have a deeper union with him and know the joy of being called into his family. If we just step out in faith, as the hemorrhaging woman did, God will pour out his grace and multiply our faith. We can see miracles in our day.

God's grace is always enough for us. We need only reach out to him as this woman did and as the official did on behalf of his daughter. How can we reach out to Jesus? By coming into his presence in prayer and allowing him to speak to us. The closer we come to Jesus, the more we will experience his healing touch upon our lives. Let us not be afraid or ashamed to tell him our needs. The reason he came into the world was to save us and restore us. As we step out in faith, he will raise us up in the same way he raised the official's daughter from the dead.

"Lord Jesus, thank you for your desire to work powerfully in our lives and bring us closer to your Father. Teach us to step out in faith and experience your healing touch. Strengthen our faith by your grace so that we may know you more deeply."

Luke 9:1-6

1 And he called the twelve together and gave them power
and authority over all demons and to cure diseases, 2 and he
sent them out to preach the kingdom of God and to heal.
3 And he said to them, "Take nothing for your journey, no staff,
nor bag, nor bread, nor money; and do not have two tunics.
4 And whatever house you enter, stay there, and from there
depart. 5 And wherever they do not receive you, when you leave
that town shake off the dust from your feet as a testimony
against them." 6 And they departed and went through the
villages, preaching the gospel and healing everywhere.

As Jesus began to move toward Jerusalem, he brought the mission in Galilee to a close by sending out the twelve to proclaim the gospel and to heal the sick. Were they ready? Were they fully prepared and qualified?

It is interesting to note that even in this story of the disciples' mission, Jesus remains at the center. It was Jesus who "called the twelve together" (Luke 9:1), just as he had initially called each disciple to come and follow him. Over time, Jesus had revealed himself and shared his life with them. These were not self-appointed apostles, and they certainly were not natural power-houses of charisma and capability! The only thing that distinguished them was their relationship to Jesus.

Before he sent them out, Jesus gave his apostles "power and authority over all demons and to cure diseases" (Luke 9:1). Everything came from Jesus. The apostles were not schooled in theology, and they didn't have a lot of experience in healing and exorcism. On the contrary, they seem to have been easily frightened and lacking in faith. Yet, Jesus gave them power and authority over both physical and spiritual realities! In describing Jesus' commissioning of these men, Luke used the Greek word *apostello*, which means "one who is sent by another." The apostles did not volunteer for the mission with any sense of confidence or conviction. They were simply sent to witness to who Jesus is, and to testify to God's power through their actions.

It is no different today. The same Jesus who called the twelve calls each of us personally. This same Jesus gives us authority over demons and sickness today. This same Jesus sends us out to proclaim a simple and uncomplicated gospel of the kingdom of God, to heal the physically and spiritually wounded, and to love as unconditionally as he does. We do not go forth on the basis of our abilities, our perfection, or our powers, but simply in the name and power of Jesus Christ. The Master has chosen us and equipped us to do his will by the power of his Spirit living within us.

"Lord, help us to recognize your call, to receive your power and authority, and to be faithful in proclaiming the kingdom of God. By your Spirit, may we extend your gift of healing to all of your children."

Luke 9:7-9

7 Now Herod the tetrarch heard of all that was done, and he
was perplexed, because it was said by some that John had been
raised from the dead, 8 by some that Elijah had appeared, and by
others that one of the old prophets had risen. 9 Herod said,
"John I beheaded; but who is this about whom I hear such
things?" And he sought to see him.

Herod had John the Baptist executed to free himself from John's message of repentance and reconciliation to God. John spoke the word of God so clearly that Herod was convicted of his sin, particularly his illicit marriage to his sister-in-law (Luke 3:19-20). Instead of turning to God in repentance, Herod killed John, hoping that the message would be buried with the messenger.

To Herod's consternation, however, the message lived on—even more powerfully—in Jesus and his disciples. If killing the messenger did not destroy the message, how could he ever escape? Herod was confused because nothing of this world could prevent God's message of salvation from being proclaimed. Later, we read that Herod was once again faced with the choice between listening to the messenger or putting him to death to silence the message (Luke 23:7-12). Instead of learning from his experience with John the Baptist, Herod chose to be part of Jesus' crucifixion. We can only imagine how confused Herod was when news of Jesus' resurrection reached him.

In both instances, Herod saw what happens when the power of God transforms death into life. It was God's power that enabled John the Baptist to remain faithful to his call, even to his death. It was the same divine power that enabled Jesus to forgive his persecutors and raised him from the dead and seated him at the Father's right hand. This is the power that fell on the disciples at Pentecost and enabled them to proclaim the gospel with boldness and confidence. Age after age, God has acted in power, building his kingdom through his servants. And, age after age, some have sought—to no avail—to silence the message of salvation by silencing its messengers.

Just as the twelve went about doing the exact same works that Jesus had done, we too can become like our Master. No matter how much opposition we may face, if we resolve, like Jesus, to love everyone and forgive every offense, his kingdom will advance. Let us ask the Spirit to make us more like Jesus, proclaiming the good news of salvation wherever we go.

"Jesus, we want to glorify you in all that we say or do. By your Spirit, empower us to turn away from sin and embrace your life so that we can become more and more like you."

Luke 9:10-17

10 On their return the apostles told him what they had done.
And he took them and withdrew apart to a city called Beth-
saida. 11 When the crowds learned it, they followed him; and he
welcomed them and spoke to them of the kingdom of God, and
cured those who had need of healing. 12 Now the day began to
wear away; and the twelve came and said to him, "Send the
crowd away, to go into the villages and country round about, to
lodge and get provisions; for we are here in a lonely place."
13 But he said to them, "You give them something to eat." They
said, "We have no more than five loaves and two fish—unless we
are to go and buy food for all these people." 14 For there were
about five thousand men. And he said to his disciples, "Make
them sit down in companies, about fifty each." 15 And they did
so, and made them all sit down. 16 And taking the five loaves
and the two fish he looked up to heaven, and blessed and broke
them, and gave them to the disciples to set before the crowd.
17 And all ate and were satisfied. And they took up what was left
over, twelve baskets of broken pieces.

In recounting the feeding of the 5,000, Luke tells how Jesus had intended to withdraw with his apostles for rest, but instead welcomed the throng that crowded around him. Like a gentle shepherd, he tended to the sick, taught them about the kingdom, and miraculously provided them with food. He ministered to them until everyone was satisfied (Luke 9:17).

As he wrote to the troubled church in Corinth, St. Paul explained that Jesus is still able to care for his people: "As often as you eat this bread and drink the cup, you proclaim the Lord's death until he comes" (1 Corinthians 11:26). Every time we read the scriptures, we can be refreshed. Every time we pray, we can be filled with the Holy Spirit. Jesus' sacrifice—which we recall at every Mass—still has the power to wash away our sins and fill us with divine life.

The bread and wine transformed into Jesus' body and blood can truly sustain us as we approach his altar with humble hearts. At the same time, whenever we eat and drink, we also look for the day when Jesus will come again. Then, he himself will feed us directly, no longer through word and sacrament. "He will wipe away every tear from their eyes, and death shall be no more, neither shall there be mourning nor crying nor pain any more, for the former things have passed away" (Revelation 21:4).

Today, let us eat and drink of Jesus with grateful hearts. It is he who feeds us. It is he who can meet all our physical and spiritual needs. Let us look for the day when Jesus will be with us. All of our hope is centered on it.

"O Lord, in your words, we find truth. In your wounds, we find life. In your precious blood, we find the power to draw near to you. In your death, we find life. In your resurrection, we find hope for eternal life. Come, Lord Jesus."

Luke 9:18-22

18 Now it happened that as he was praying alone the disciples
were with him; and he asked them, "Who do the people say that
I am?" 19 And they answered, "John the Baptist; but others say,
Elijah; and others, that one of the old prophets has risen." 20 And
he said to them, "But who do you say that I am?" And Peter
answered, "The Christ of God." 21 But he charged and commanded
them to tell this to no one, 22 saying, "The Son of man must
suffer many things, and be rejected by the elders and chief priests
and scribes, and be killed, and on the third day be raised."

In one of the most famous conversations in scripture, Jesus asked his apostles: "Who do you say that I am?" In reply, Peter said: "The Christ of God" (Luke 9:20). With this confession, nothing would be the same. Having seen Jesus perform numerous miracles throughout Galilee, the apostles would now begin their journey to Jerusalem where "the Son of man must suffer many things, and be rejected by the elders and chief priests and scribes, and be killed, and on the third day be raised" (9:22).

Luke tells us that just before this conversation, Jesus had been praying alone with his disciples (Luke 9:18). Throughout his gospel, in fact, Luke portrays Jesus as being absorbed in prayer just before important events occur. At his baptism, Jesus was praying when the Holy Spirit descended upon him (3:21-22). Jesus prayed all night long before he chose his twelve apostles (6:12-13). It was in prayer that Jesus was transfigured (9:28-30). Finally, as his passion was about to unfold, Jesus unburdened his heart to his Father in prayer (22:39-46). Throughout the gospel, we see Jesus relying on God's wisdom and power.

When Jesus asked his disciples who they said he was, he was not just challenging them, but inviting them into a deeper relationship with him. He wanted them to learn to open their hearts to God in prayer and receive his life and his love. In the book of Acts, Luke tells us that as the apostles learned how to pray, they became effective ministers of the gospel, understanding God's purposes and willingly laying down their lives for the sake of the kingdom (see Acts 4:23-31; 10:9-48; 27:21-26).

Jesus invites all of us to come to know him in prayer. He has already worked wonders in our lives, yet in his generosity, he wants to give us much more. As we behold his glory in prayer, he will fill our hearts with awe and gratitude. The Holy Spirit will reveal Jesus to us. He will change our hearts and teach us how to know God's presence throughout our days.

"Come, Lord, and fill us with a longing to know you. By the power of your Spirit, enkindle in our hearts a burning desire for your revelation. As we pray, open our eyes to see your glory and your perfection."

Luke 9:23-27

23 And he said to all, "If any man would come after me, let him
deny himself and take up his cross daily and follow me. 24 For
whoever would save his life will lose it; and whoever loses his life
for my sake, he will save it. 25 For what does it profit a man if he
gains the whole world and loses or forfeits himself? 26 For
whoever is ashamed of me and of my words, of him will the Son
of man be ashamed when he comes in his glory and the glory of
the Father and of the holy angels. 27 But I tell you truly, there
are some standing here who will not taste death before they see
the kingdom of God."

Nothing can sound less appealing than the call to take up our cross and follow Jesus every day (Luke 9:23). We instinctively imagine a life of suffering and self-denial. True, death to self is part of following the Lord, but only if we look at life with Jesus from a solely human perspective will we feel frustrated by the prospect.

Each of us—whether we believe in God or not—thirsts for the Lord. How often have we felt like the psalmist—weary and needy, longing for God's presence (see Psalm 63:1). Yet, when we seek the Lord, we encounter a conflict between our desire for Jesus and our desire to remain in sin. This very conflict, in part, illustrates the "cross" that we are called to take up. God asks us to crucify our sinful drives so that we can find our true home in Jesus.

How do we approach Jesus' words with hope, not fear? The key is in exchanging our limited perspective, which looks only at what we lose, for the greater truth of who Jesus is and what he offers us. The more we truly lay down our lives, the more we allow Jesus to pour his life into us.

We can take up the cross by deciding to seek Jesus in prayer every day. Prayer can be like going to a friend's wedding. If we only think of the traffic we will encounter on the way, we'll find it hard to get into the car. But if we consider the wonderful celebration and the banquet awaiting us, we gladly fight the traffic. It will be worth it to us. Or perhaps there is a person in our lives whom we wish we could avoid. Again, as we obey the Lord's promptings to lay down our lives, we will be filled with divine love and receive the grace to share that love. Let us embrace the life God has called us to. It may be difficult at times, but the rewards far outweigh the costs!

"Jesus, one glimpse of your beauty makes the fight worthwhile. Help me to keep my eyes fixed fully on you as I take up my cross and follow you."

Luke 9:28-36

28 Now about eight days after these sayings he took with him
Peter and John and James, and went up on the mountain to pray.
29 And as he was praying, the appearance of his countenance was
altered, and his raiment became dazzling white. 30 And behold,
two men talked with him, Moses and Elijah, 31 who appeared in
glory and spoke of his departure, which he was to accomplish at
Jerusalem. 32 Now Peter and those who were with him were
heavy with sleep, but kept awake and they saw his glory and the
two men who stood with him. 33 And as the men were parting
from him, Peter said to Jesus, "Master, it is well that we are here;
let us make three booths, one for you and one for Moses and one
for Elijah"—not knowing what he said. 34 As he said this, a
cloud came and overshadowed them; and they were afraid as
they entered the cloud. 35 And a voice came out of the cloud,
saying, "This is my Son, my Chosen; listen to him!"
36 And when the voice had spoken, Jesus was found alone. And
they kept silence and told no one in those days anything of what
they had seen.

What a multitude of thoughts must have filled the minds of Peter, James, and John as they reflected on Jesus' words about his suffering, his rejection by his own people, his coming death and resurrection (Luke 9:22-24). Now on the mountain with Jesus to pray, these same apostles would face the glorious moment of Jesus' transfiguration.

The radiance of divine glory was about to be displayed before their eyes as a confirmation of all that Jesus had taught them about himself as the Messiah of God, the Son of Man (Luke 9:20,22). Their experience would serve as a means of changing their hearts about what they then considered the shame and humiliation of the cross. It was a pledge of Christ's future glory to be shared with all those who faithfully follow his way (9:23-27).

Glory is an attribute of God. It is God himself revealed in his majesty, goodness, power and holiness (see Psalm 96:7-9). It is the reflection of his love for his people. Glory is seen in the faithfulness of God's promise to Abraham (see Genesis 15:17-18), in the splendor shining on Moses' face after he had spoken with Yahweh (see Exodus 34:29), and in the wonder of his mark on the world he created (see Isaiah 6:3). It is associated with the tabernacle and the temple (see Exodus 40:34; 1 Kings 8:10-11), with cloud by day and fire by night (see Exodus 13:21), and with the visions of the prophets (see Isaiah 60:1-2; Ezekiel 10:4). Jesus is the fullness of God's glory. He is the Lord of glory (see 1 Corinthians 2:8), and the radiant light of God's glory (see Hebrews 1:3).

For Jesus, the cross was the entrance into the Father's glory. Having endured the cross, he now reigns gloriously forever in the heavenly courts. Jesus has promised us a share in this same glory when he transfigures our bodies to reflect his own glorious body (see Philippians 3:17,21). But the only way to experience such glory is in fellowship with the cross of Jesus, by more and more surrendering our lives to him, faithfully obeying the Father's command to "listen to him" (Luke 9:35), and by humbly submitting to his will for our lives.

Today in prayer ask for a deeper understanding of the glory of the cross, a growing awareness of God's presence among us, and the desire to embrace and remain always in that glorious presence.

Luke 9:37-45

[37] On the next day, when they had come down from the
mountain, a great crowd met him. [38] And behold, a man from
the crowd cried, "Teacher, I beg you to look upon my son, for he
is my only child; [39] and behold, a spirit seizes him, and he
suddenly cries out; it convulses him till he foams, and shatters
him, and will hardly leave him. [40] And I begged your disciples to
cast it out, but they could not." [41] Jesus answered, "O faithless
and perverse generation, how long am I to be with you and bear
with you? Bring your son here." [42] While he was coming, the
demon tore him and convulsed him. But Jesus rebuked the
unclean spirit, and healed the boy, and gave him back to his
father. [43] And all were astonished at the majesty of God.
But while they were all marveling at everything he did, he
said to his disciples, [44] "Let these words sink into your ears; for
the Son of man is to be delivered into the hands of men." [45] But
they did not understand this saying, and it was concealed from
them, that they should not perceive it; and they were afraid to
ask him about this saying.

What if modern medicine were somehow able to end all suffering due to sickness and disease? It would be a cause for great rejoicing, certainly, but, by faith, we know it would not address our spiritual needs. Only the cross of Christ can deal with the heart's desire for God. In a way, Luke made this point by juxtaposing a miracle story with Jesus' second prediction about his passion. When Jesus healed a demon-possessed boy (Luke 9:38-42), "all were astonished at the majesty of God. But while they were all marveling at everything he did, he said to his disciples, 'Let these words sink into your ears; for the Son of Man is to be delivered into the hands of men'" (9:43-44).

Once again, Jesus revealed the central reality of his mission to all who would be his disciples: The cross is the way of salvation and eternal life. Discipleship, union with God, fullness of life—these things come not as a result of miracles or teachings, but through obedience to Jesus' call. "If any man would come after me, let him deny himself and take up his cross daily and follow me" (Luke 9:23).

Because of their faith, the disciples were able to go out "preaching the gospel and healing everyone" (Luke 9:6). That was the fruit of their calling, but not its essence. Full discipleship means allowing the cross of Christ to separate us from sin and conform us more and more into the image of God's Son.

This was the second time Jesus predicted his passion to the disciples, but once more "they did not understand" (Luke 9:45). In the end, they had to experience Jesus' resurrection in order to grasp the significance of his cross. The same holds true for us. It is only by the power of the Holy Spirit that we will come to experience the great freedom and hope available to us as we allow the cross of Christ to put to death the ways of sin within us. Let us ask the Spirit to open our minds and our hearts to the power that can flow from union with Jesus' death and resurrection.

"Lord God, write the message of the cross on our hearts, that we might seek to mature in the life in the Spirit through your Son's victory over sin and death."

Luke 9:46-50

46 And an argument arose among them as to which of them was
the greatest. 47 But when Jesus perceived the thought of their
hearts, he took a child and put him by his side, 48 and said to
them, "Whoever receives this child in my name receives me, and
whoever receives me receives him who sent me; for he who is least
among you all is the one who is great."
49 John answered, "Master, we saw a man casting out demons in
your name, and we forbade him, because he does not follow with
us." 50 But Jesus said to him, "Do not forbid him; for he that is not
against you is for you."

The disciples had seen Jesus preach, heal, and perform miracles and exorcisms. Giving them authority over demons and the power to cure diseases, Jesus had also sent them out to preach the kingdom of God and to heal (Luke 9:1-2). Knowing the human tendency to let power go to our head, is it any wonder that the disciples began to argue about which one of them was the greatest?

The fact that these disciples, who were so close to the Lord, fell into competition with one another might cause us to wonder whether it is possible for us to take on the childlike humility and dependence on God that Jesus taught. "He who is least among you all is the one who is great" (Luke 9:48). But the first disciples' experience can actually teach us the opposite lesson. They learned from their failures. By the power of the Holy Spirit, they grew in the humility they needed for their role of service for the kingdom of God.

From the moment of his conception, Jesus led a life of complete humility. His taking on human nature was itself the most astounding act of humility: He "did not count equality with God a thing to be grasped, but emptied himself, taking the form of a servant" (Philippians 2:6-7). He humbly let the Father be all in everything he did (see John 5:19). In humility he submitted even to the cross.

The secret of becoming humble lies in Jesus himself. To those of us who find ourselves burdened with pride and self-concern, Jesus says "Take my yoke upon you, and learn from me" (Matthew 11:29). So we are on the way to humility as we meditate on Jesus' words to his disciples. We are on the way as we praise and worship him and draw near to his love for us. The key to humility lies in the abiding presence of Jesus, the Humble One, in our hearts. Let us turn to him often during the day and say, "Make me like you, Jesus."

"Jesus, help us to abide in the communion with God which we lost through our sin but was restored to us through your humble death and resurrection. Through this communion may we gain the humility that you desire for us."

The Meaning of Discipleship

Luke
9:51–11:54

Luke 9:51-56

51 When the days drew near for him to be received up, he set
his face to go to Jerusalem. 52 And he sent messengers ahead
of him, who went and entered a village of the Samaritans, to
make ready for him; 53 but the people would not receive him,
because his face was set toward Jerusalem. 54 And when his
disciples James and John saw it, they said, "Lord, do you want
us to bid fire come down from heaven and consume them?" 55
But he turned and rebuked them. 56 And they went on to
another village.

Because the time of his passion and death were drawing near, Jesus "set his face" against all hostilities and opposition "to go to Jerusalem" (Luke 9:51). His time in Galilee had come to a close, and the time had come to bring his disciples with him on the way of the cross. And, as in the beginning of his Galilean ministry (4:14-30), Jesus again experienced rejection (9:52-56)—yet another foreshadowing of the rejection he would encounter in Jerusalem.

One of Luke's recurring themes is Jesus' mercy toward sinners and outcasts, and the Jews considered Samaritans to be both. This helps us understand why Jesus chose to travel through Samaria. He was certainly aware that Jewish pilgrims who passed this way often faced Samaritan hostilities. Yet, his desire to reach out to the rejected and despised moved Jesus to risk the route.

When a certain Samaritan town "would not receive him because his face was set toward Jerusalem" (Luke 9:53), Jesus reacted peacefully and with patience. James and John, on the other hand, sought retaliation. This gave Jesus an opportunity to teach his disciples forgiveness in the face of rejection, and love in the face of hatred. The Son of Man came not to be served but to serve. He will never force himself on anyone, much though their rejection might hurt him.

When we are faced with rejection, how do we respond? Often, in our wounded pride, we strike out, seeking to restore our sense of honor. But Jesus taught that true honor comes not from others' opinions of us, but only from the fact that we are loved and accepted by God. Through the gift of faith and by the grace in the sacraments, we too are called to travel with Jesus toward the cross. In him, we will find all we need to sustain us as we face difficulty, opposition, and trials along the way. Every day, let us recall and thank God for our inheritance as beloved brothers and sisters of Christ. Let us ask the Spirit to replace any desires for retaliation with Jesus' heart of mercy and compassion.

"Lord Jesus, fill our minds with all that you have done for us by your sacrifice on the cross. Heal our memories of rejection, and fill us with your love so that we can face any opposition with your love."

Luke 9:57-62

57 As they were going along the road, a man said to him, "I will
follow you wherever you go." 58 And Jesus said to him, "Foxes
have holes, and birds of the air have nests; but the Son of man
has nowhere to lay his head." 59 To another he said, "Follow me."
But he said, "Lord, let me first go and bury my father." 60 But he
said to him, "Leave the dead to bury their own dead; but as for
you, go and proclaim the kingdom of God." 61 Another said, "I
will follow you, Lord; but let me first say farewell to those at my
home." 62 Jesus said to him, "No one who puts his hand to the
plow and looks back is fit for the kingdom of God."

As Jesus began his final journey to Jerusalem, he sought to gather together a group of disciples whom he could teach and form along the way. For some, the calling was a great privilege and adventure. For others, it posed too great a challenge, and so they gave understandable reasons for delaying their response. Who among us today would forego our father's funeral, or fail to say good-bye to our family, simply because we wanted to follow a popular preacher to his date with destiny?

Throughout his gospel, Luke places significant emphasis on the cost of discipleship. When we set out to follow Jesus, we often do not know what we are getting ourselves into. There will be times when we are called to go against the tide of prevailing philosophies, and there is the constant battle between flesh and spirit that has its moments of particular fierceness. Numerous saints and holy people have witnessed to the fact that the call to become like our Master includes both the cross and the resurrection.

Why would we want to take up such a calling? Only the experience of Jesus' great love in rescuing us from darkness can compel us sufficiently. We keep this love alive by prayer, communion with Jesus, and repentance as soon as we are aware that we have separated ourselves from God's will. These simple acts demonstrate our willingness to be disciples and open us to the constant care of the Holy Spirit. A simple prayer in the midst of a busy day can avail us of our Father's love when we feel empty, of his mercy when we disobey him, and of his warm embrace when we return to him.

The call is costly at times, but the rewards are great. Consider the privilege of leading a person away from sin through our prayer, or through gentle cajoling! Think of the joy we have when we share our faith and bring others closer to Jesus. The call to discipleship is fraught with challenges, but we can always take comfort in the knowledge that God is with us and is working to make us into vessels of his healing power as we remain close to him.

"Lord Jesus, we ask you for the grace to seek your will every day, the wisdom to recognize it, and the power to move in accord with your grace. By your Spirit within us, make us into your disciples."

Luke 10:1-12

1 After this the Lord appointed seventy others, and sent them
on ahead of him, two by two, into every town and place where
he himself was about to come. 2 And he said to them, "The
harvest is plentiful, but the laborers are few; pray therefore the
Lord of the harvest to send out laborers into his harvest. 3 Go
your way; behold, I send you out as lambs in the midst of wolves.
4 Carry no purse, no bag, no sandals; and salute no one on the
road. 5 Whatever house you enter, first say, 'Peace be to this
house!' 6 And if a son of peace is there, your peace shall rest
upon him; but if not, it shall return to you. 7 And remain in the
same house, eating and drinking what they provide, for the
laborer deserves his wages; do not go from house to house.
8 Whenever you enter a town and they receive you, eat what is
set before you; 9 heal the sick in it and say to them, 'The
kingdom of God has come near to you.' 10 But whenever you
enter a town and they do not receive you, go into its streets and
say, 11 'Even the dust of your town that clings to our feet, we
wipe off against you; nevertheless know this, that the kingdom of
God has come near.' 12 I tell you, it shall be more tolerable on
that day for Sodom than for that town."

In his instructions to the seventy disciples, Jesus provided detailed guidelines on how they were to conduct their mission. These guidelines apply to us as well. We are called to put the service of God first, to remove any obstacles or distractions that might prevent us from fulfilling our mission. We are to proclaim the peace of Christ by allowing our example to infect others with the desire to love.

"Mission" can mean many things. It can mean honoring and praising God right where you are, thanking him for all he has given us in Christ. It can mean bringing our children to know Jesus. If we are young, it can mean caring for the old. If we are older, it can mean praying for the young. It can involve writing to lawmakers in objection to legislation that is in direct violation of God's plan. It can mean bearing witness to the lordship of Jesus in our daily lives. Any deed performed in love and joy can be a way of fulfilling our mission here on earth.

St. Luke was one disciple who experienced what it meant to be commissioned by God. Even though he was not a direct witness of the life and preaching of the Lord, he understood that from baptism on, every Christian is called to a mission—to respond to the Spirit's promptings, however small or large. Scripture depicts Luke joining Paul at Troas and accompanying him in missionary work to Philippi (see Acts 16:6-12). The second letter of Timothy refers to Luke as Paul's only companion during his imprisonment in Rome (see 2 Timothy 4:11); the letter to Philemon mentions Luke as one of Paul's "fellow workers" (Philemon 24). St. Luke wrote not only the Gospel but the book of Acts as well. Through these writings, his mission continues to this day.

It is often thought that "mission" applies only to those who are young, zealous, vigorous, and who are willing to travel to far away places. This can be a limiting view of God's grand plan for the church. Neither St. Luke nor the seventy disciples were unique in their qualifications. What equipped them for service was their awareness of Jesus' power, love, and his vision for all humanity.

God has a mission for each one of us. As we listen carefully to the Holy Spirit, he will reveal his plan for our lives.

Luke 10:13-16

13 "Woe to you, Chorazin! woe to you, Beth-saida! for if the
mighty works done in you had been done in Tyre and Sidon,
they would have repented long ago, sitting in sackcloth and
ashes. 14 But it shall be more tolerable in the judgment for Tyre
and Sidon than for you. 15 And you, Caperna-um, will you be
exalted to heaven? You shall be brought down to Hades.
16 "He who hears you hears me, and he who rejects you rejects
me, and he who rejects me rejects him who sent me."

Jesus had just instructed his disciples about their mission. They were to go ahead of him into the towns that he would visit and prepare the people for his arrival by healing the sick, casting out demons, and proclaiming the kingdom of God. Perhaps to impress on his disciples the gravity of their task, Jesus concluded his instructions by making it clear just whose message they would be speaking and how much would depend on people's responses.

Jesus had come as God's spokesman to extend God's offer of life and peace; now, in turn, he was sending his disciples to speak for him (Luke 10:16). Thus, to accept or reject the disciples' message would be to accept or reject God himself. Those who heard the disciples would face the most important choice of their lives; their eternal destiny depended on how they responded. Jesus' lamentations over the fate of towns that had already rejected him

(10:13-15) must have left the disciples feeling quite sober about the task he was entrusting to them.

As members of Jesus' body, we all share in the calling "to spread the kingdom of Christ over all the earth" (*Catechism of the Catholic Church*, 863). Each of us has a particular mission field: our family, our workplace, our neighborhood. The fate of the people with whom we live and work is very important to God. To equip us for such a challenging mission, Jesus offers us a share in his very life—through prayer, his word, and his presence in the Eucharist (see CCC, 864).

Do you know someone who is far from the Lord? It's never too late for him or her. Pray for those who are lost. Intercede that the Spirit of revelation would be released in their lives. Bind them to Jesus. Loose them from the effects of the Evil One. If you feel that God is calling you to witness to them, do so in a spirit of love and compassion. Show them that the gospel is the most hopeful, and most powerful, message in the world.

"Lord, fill me with your love so that I may love others. Give me your desire that others would come to know you. Use me to make yourself known to them. Draw men and women into your kingdom."

Luke 10:17-24

17 The seventy returned with joy, saying, "Lord, even the demons
are subject to us in your name!" 18 And he said to them, "I saw
Satan fall like lightning from heaven. 19 Behold, I have given
you authority to tread upon serpents and scorpions, and over all
the power of the enemy; and nothing shall hurt you.
20 Nevertheless do not rejoice in this, that the spirits are subject
to you; but rejoice that your names are written in heaven."
21 In that same hour he rejoiced in the Holy Spirit and said, "I

thank thee, Father, Lord of heaven and earth, that thou
hast hidden these things from the wise and understanding and revealed them to babes; yea, Father, for such was
thy gracious will. [22] All things have been delivered to me
by my Father; and no one knows who the Son is except
the Father, or who the Father is except the Son and any
one to whom the Son chooses to reveal him."
23 Then turning to the disciples he said privately,
"Blessed are the eyes which see what you see! [24] For I tell
you that many prophets and kings desired to see what
you see, and did not see it, and to hear what you hear,
and did not hear it."

Jesus was filled with the Holy Spirit (see Matthew 3:16). Full of joy, he prayed to his Father in gratitude because his disciples were beginning to understand the truths of God. He thanked the Father for his gracious love, for while these things remained hidden "from the wise and the intelligent," they were revealed to "infants" (Luke 10:21). That is, those who took delight in their own intelligence did not understand, but those who trusted God began to grasp the truth.

Isaiah had prophesied that the Messiah would be the one on whom the Spirit would rest (see Isaiah 11:2-3). Jesus revealed the indwelling Spirit through the work he did and the joy he experienced. The Holy Spirit longs to reveal Jesus in a way which would excite our faith and give us this same joy. We can expect this because we have the same Spirit given to us through baptism and faith.

Our Father wants the great truths of our faith to come alive for us; he wants us to know the joy which comes from being filled with the Spirit. One of the roles of the Holy Spirit is to reveal to us who Jesus is (see John 16:12-13). On a practical note, how do we open ourselves to the work of God in us? It means carving out a time and space to be with the Lord in prayer, being present in body and spirit at the liturgy, and asking the Spirit to teach us about Jesus. It means taking time to read scripture and asking the Spirit to bring it to life for us—to hear the word of God.

Ask the Holy Spirit to work in you in a deeper and exciting way. Ask him to open up the profound truth in God's word and enliven your prayer so that you can be transformed. Ask him to help you trust him with your life.

"Heavenly Father, open my mind to the work of the Spirit within me. May I respond to his promptings so that I will perceive and grasp in a deeper way the truth that God is with us through Christ Jesus. Help my trust in you to grow."

Luke 10:25-37

25 And behold, a lawyer stood up to put him to the test, saying,
"Teacher, what shall I do to inherit eternal life?"
26 He said to
him, "What is written in the law? How do you read?"
27 And he
answered, "You shall love the Lord your God with all your heart,
and with all your soul, and with all your strength, and with all
your mind; and your neighbor as yourself."
28 And he said to
him, "You have answered right; do this, and you will live."
29 But he, desiring to justify himself, said to Jesus, "And who is
my neighbor?"
30 Jesus replied, "A man was going down from
Jerusalem to Jericho, and he fell among robbers, who stripped
him and beat him, and departed, leaving him half dead.
31 Now
by chance a priest was going down that road; and when he saw
him he passed by on the other side.
32 So likewise a Levite, when

he came to the place and saw him, passed by on the other side.
33 But a Samaritan, as he journeyed, came to where he was; and
when he saw him, he had compassion, 34 and went to him and
bound up his wounds, pouring on oil and wine; then he set him
on his own beast and brought him to an inn, and took care of
him. 35 And the next day he took out two denarii and gave them
to the innkeeper, saying, 'Take care of him; and whatever more
you spend, I will repay you when I come back.' 36 Which of
these three, do you think, proved neighbor to the man who fell
among the robbers?" 37 He said, "The one who showed mercy on
him." And Jesus said to him, "Go and do likewise."

Picture in your mind someone you find particularly hard to deal with: an overbearing boss, a self-righteous relative, an especially rude neighbor. If we are honest, we have to admit that we set limits on whom we love. Less dramatically, we allow considerations of who is currently in or out of power, or who is part of our group or an outsider, to determine whom we will love.

The Jews of Jesus' day were no different. To them, "neighbor" meant a fellow Israelite. This made Jesus' statement all the more startling: All people become neighbors in the kingdom of God. Jesus came to draw all people to himself (see John 12:32). This non-exclusivity was demonstrated vividly by whom he called to himself: coarse fishermen, greedy tax collectors, prostitutes. In Jesus' view, everyone is our neighbor.

To love one's neighbor is to abolish all boundaries, all divisions. It means seeing things from the other person's point of view and responding to that without regard to outward appearances. The parable of the good Samaritan shows this. The Samaritan stopped to help a man who had been robbed, stripped and beaten because he saw the man's need—and was moved by that consideration alone.

The lawyer who questioned Jesus knew that the law could be summarized as loving God and loving neighbor (Luke 10:27). Jesus challenged him: "You have answered right; do this, and you will live." (10:28). That challenge is for us, too. But rather than try to justify ourselves, let us cry out, "How? How can I possibly fulfill what God intends, that I love even those whom I find objectionable?" This is the response Jesus sought. The answer to our cry is, "You can't, but in God you can."

God saved us through Jesus and continually gives us life through him. God does the work. It does not depend on us, but on him. How often—like the lawyer, the priest, and the Levite—we try to reduce God's command to love to something less than it really is. We want to hold on to restrictions which rule out situations that make us uncomfortable or stretch us beyond our own natural abilities. Thus we rule out the love we are commanded to show.

Jesus was calling for something far greater than we can accomplish on our own. Only in Christ can we truly love others, or wholeheartedly love God. And that is as incredible as a Samaritan fulfilling the law.

Luke 10:38-42

38 Now as they went on their way, he entered a village; and a
woman named Martha received him into her house. 39 And she
had a sister called Mary, who sat at the Lord's feet and listened to
his teaching. 40 But Martha was distracted with much serving;
and she went to him and said, "Lord, do you not care that my
sister has left me to serve alone? Tell her then to help me."
41 But the Lord answered her, "Martha, Martha, you are anxious
and troubled about many things; 42 one thing is needful. Mary
has chosen the good portion, which shall not be taken away
from her."

Our friends are very important to us. In addition to being a source of pleasure, they are crucial to our spiritual, emotional, and physical well-being. Through friendship we learn how to trust, love, and respect each other; we learn how to give and receive encouragement. Jesus also knew the importance of friendships, and he found real friends in Lazarus and his sisters—Mary and Martha. He was always welcome in their home, and as he relaxed with them, he taught them about the kingdom of God. As a result of their friendship with Jesus, these three were touched and began to place their faith and trust in him as the Son of God. As a result, their lives were never the same.

Unlike her sister Mary, who put everything aside to sit at Jesus' feet and listen to him, Martha was distracted by her responsibilities as a hostess. Because of their friendship, Martha was able to be honest with Jesus about feeling overworked, and Jesus was able to correct her (Luke 10:40-42). Martha perhaps did not understand at first that she was in the presence of the Son of God! If she had, she probably would have been sitting at Jesus' feet as well, basking in his presence like her sister Mary.

In her heart, however, Martha must have pondered Jesus' words because her faith grew as a result of his correction. When she met Jesus following her brother's death, Martha demonstrated a real growth in faith. Even though Lazarus had died, she knew that God would answer Jesus' prayers (see John 11:22). When Jesus asked her if she believed that all who believe in him would have eternal life, she was able to reply: "Yes, Lord, I believe that you are the Christ, the Son of God, he who is coming into the world" (11:27).

Jesus wants to have a close friendship with all of us. Let us invite him to refresh us and teach us every day as we pray, ponder his word, and participate in the life of the church. As we come to know him, we too will be conformed to his likeness, just as Martha was.

"Jesus, we welcome you into our hearts. Abide with us and teach us who you are more intimately each day. Transform our lives by your presence so that we too can see your glory and be raised to new life in you."

Luke 11:1-13

1 He was praying in a certain place, and when he ceased, one
of his disciples said to him, "Lord, teach us to pray, as John taught
his disciples." 2 And he said to them, "When you pray, say:
"Father, hallowed be thy name. Thy kingdom come. 3 Give
us each day our daily bread; 4 and forgive us our sins, for we
ourselves forgive every one who is indebted to us; and lead us not
into temptation."
5 And he said to them, "Which of you who has a friend will go
to him at midnight and say to him, 'Friend, lend me three loaves;
6 for a friend of mine has arrived on a journey, and I have
nothing to set before him'; 7 and he will answer from within,
'Do not bother me; the door is now shut, and my children are
with me in bed; I cannot get up and give you anything'? 8 I tell
you, though he will not get up and give him anything because he
is his friend, yet because of his importunity he will rise and give
him whatever he needs. 9 And I tell you, Ask, and it will be
given you; seek, and you will find; knock, and it will be opened
to you. 10 For every one who asks receives, and he who seeks
finds, and to him who knocks it will be opened. 11 What father
among you, if his son asks for a fish, will instead of a fish give
him a serpent; 12 or if he asks for an egg, will give him a
scorpion? 13 If you then, who are evil, know how to give good
gifts to your children, how much more will the heavenly Father
give the Holy Spirit to those who ask him!"

How much more will the heavenly Father give the Holy Spirit to those who ask him! (Luke 11:13)

Have you ever wondered why Jesus ended this sermon with a reference to the Holy Spirit? After telling his disciples the kinds of things a son might ask of his father, he suddenly said how the Father delights in giving the Holy Spirit to those who ask. Why this above all the other things for which we might pray? If we look at what scripture says about the Holy Spirit, we can see that the Spirit is indeed a most precious gift God gives, one through which we receive all the blessings of the Lord's Prayer.

We can ask that the Father's name be worshipped (hallowed), but Jesus wants us to know that it is the Spirit who glorifies him as he lives in his followers (see John 16:12-14). When we pray for forgiveness and to be kept from temptation, we are praying that the Spirit come into our hearts, convict us of sin, and lead us into all truth so that we can recognize and avoid the wiles of the devil and the empty allure of the world (see John 14:15-17; 16:8-11).

The Spirit reveals to us the glory, the majesty, the grace, and love of our Savior. He gives us knowledge of the things of God, opening our eyes to the truths of scripture, and forming our minds on the basis of these truths (see 1 Corinthians 2:10-16). Through this work of the Spirit, we are led to greater prayer and a deeper reverence for the things of God. We cannot think we are capable of producing godliness or a spiritual life apart from the work of the Spirit of Christ. Only the Spirit can produce spiritual reality (see John 3:6).

If we ask God for the Spirit, if we seek this great gift from the Father, we will not go unheard or unanswered. God works through faith, not through the emotions. The Spirit's work is not in the realm of our feelings, but in the realm of our unshakable faith, based on trust in the promises of God. Let us pray in confidence for a deepening of the work of the Spirit in us, and stand firm in faith that this great gift will teach us how to pray for all else God wishes to give us.

Luke 11:14-26

14 Now he was casting out a demon that was dumb; when the
demon had gone out, the dumb man spoke, and the people
marveled. 15 But some of them said, "He casts out demons by
Be-elzebul, the prince of demons"; 16 while others, to test him,
sought from him a sign from heaven. 17 But he, knowing their
thoughts, said to them, "Every kingdom divided against itself is
laid waste, and house falls upon house. 18 And if Satan also is
divided against himself, how will his kingdom stand? For you say
that I cast out demons by Be-elzebul. 19 And if I cast out demons
by Be-elzebul, by whom do your sons cast them out? Therefore
they shall be your judges. 20 But if it is by the finger of God that
I cast out demons, then the kingdom of God has come upon you.
21 When a strong man, fully armed, guards his own palace, his
goods are in peace; 22 but when one stronger than he assails him
and overcomes him, he takes away his armor in which he
trusted, and divides his spoil. 23 He who is not with me is against
me, and he who does not gather with me scatters.
24 "When the unclean spirit has gone out of a man, he passes
through waterless places seeking rest; and finding none he says, 'I
will return to my house from which I came.' 25 And when he
comes he finds it swept and put in order. 26 Then he goes and
brings seven other spirits more evil than himself, and they enter
and dwell there; and the last state of that man becomes worse
than the first."

When Jesus forgave the sins of the paralytic, the Jewish leaders accused him of blasphemy (Luke 5:17-26); when a sinful woman anointed Jesus, a Pharisee was upset that he allowed such a woman to touch him (7:36-50). So also when Jesus cast out a demon from the mute man (11:14), the people responded with hard hearts. Some accused him of using the power of the devil; others demanded another sign.

"But if it is by the finger of God that I cast out demons, then the kingdom of God has come upon you" (Luke 11:20). When the Israelites were in slavery in Egypt, God struck the Egyptians with plagues to force Pharaoh to let the people go free. After the plague of gnats, Pharaoh's officials said to him, "This is the finger of God!" (Exodus 8:19). They saw what they were up against! So what Jesus did when he cast out the demon from the mute man was similar to what Moses did through the plagues; both were signs of God's power working to free his people from bondage to evil.

Just as Pharaoh's heart was hard, so also were the hearts of those around Jesus. But how do we respond to the signs of God's saving power in our lives and in the lives of others? These saving works demand a response from us. Are we going to turn to the Lord and believe or not? When we do believe and resist the temptation to give in to doubt and disbelief, we will know the love of Jesus that comes from accepting him and his work among us

Jesus went on to say that the healing of the mute man was a sign that the kingdom of God had arrived. Even though the Jews didn't accept him, Jesus did establish the kingdom of God on earth through his miracles, his teaching, his death, and resurrection. Let us acknowledge that God's kingdom has broken into the world and into our own lives as well while we await the fullness of the kingdom when Jesus comes again.

"Father, teach us to recognize your work and power in the world and to turn to you in faith. We want to repent for the ways that we harden our hearts to you and don't believe. May your kingdom come."

Luke 11:27-28

27 As he said this, a woman in the crowd raised her voice and said to him, "Blessed is the womb that bore you, and the breasts that you sucked!" 28 But he said, "Blessed rather are those who hear the word of God and keep it!"

One day after Jesus had been driving out demons, debating with Pharisees, and teaching increasingly large crowds, a woman called out: "Blessed is the womb that bore you!" (Luke 11:27). You can almost hear this woman going on to say: "My, what a lucky mother to have such a son, such a great and powerful rabbi!" But Jesus responded that the truly blessed are those who "hear the word of God and keep it" (11:28).

Far from turning attention away from his mother, Jesus was showing that she was not just some lucky woman who received special graces. He understood that Mary constantly chose to lay down her life in obedience to God, and that this was the true blessing. Both the angel Gabriel and her kinswoman Elizabeth could see Mary's faith and obedience, and this was why they too called her blessed. Elizabeth said: "Blessed is she who believed that there would be a fulfillment of what was spoken to her from the Lord" (Luke 1:45).

To Gabriel, Mary said: "Let it be to me according to your word" (Luke 1:38). Consider the consequences of Mary's "yes" to the angel's extraordinary message. Imagine you are a young woman, engaged to be married, and now you are willing to accept God's will to become miraculously pregnant before you and your husband have come together. This might be a little difficult to explain to your mother and fiancé, not to mention the town gossips! Wouldn't you want to suggest that God delay the miracle until after the marriage? Does the world really need to know it was a virgin birth? Did she really have to risk being stoned to death for the sin of adultery?

Mary's act of faith and obedience is extraordinary. She deserves to be called the "New Eve," for, like Eve, she had free will, but unlike Eve, Mary trusted, believed, and obeyed. This is the woman Jesus knew as his mother. He saw her blessedness in her wisdom, strength, faith, and obedience. We too can be blessed if we seek to hear from the Lord and put his words into practice.

"Lord, you have called us into the great blessing of being your disciples. May we learn to trust and obey you just as Mary did. Help us also to count the cost, for you have said that we cannot follow you unless we deny ourselves."

Luke 11:29-32

29 When the crowds were increasing, he began to say, "This
generation is an evil generation; it seeks a sign, but no sign shall
be given to it except the sign of Jonah. 30 For as Jonah became a
sign to the men of Nineveh, so will the Son of man be to this
generation. 31 The queen of the South will arise at the judgment
with the men of this generation and condemn them; for she
came from the ends of the earth to hear the wisdom of Solomon,
and behold, something greater than Solomon is here. 32 The
men of Nineveh will arise at the judgment with this generation
and condemn it; for they repented at the preaching of Jonah,
and behold, something greater than Jonah is here."

Would it not have been easier for Jesus to give in to the people's demand for a "sign"? Surely he could have performed some amazing feat to display his divinity and silence his opposition. Jesus rebuked the crowd with harsh comparisons: "The men of Nineveh will arise at the judgment with this generation and condemn it; for they repented at the preaching of Jonah, and behold, something greater than Jonah is here" (Luke 11:32).

If only the people could have seen Jesus with eyes of faith, they would have witnessed the very sign they wanted. For the "sign of Jonah" was none other than Jesus himself. Like Jonah, he preached repentance from sins, calling God's people to reform their lives and welcome the inauguration of the kingdom of God. Through Jonah, God revealed his mercy to Nineveh, just as Jesus unveiled his Father's endless mercy to everyone who came to him in humility and repentance. Through his parables of redemption and restoration, Jesus taught us all about the prodigal love of his Father, and he lived his message of mercy every time he sat down at table with tax collectors and sinners, lepers and Samaritans.

It is worth noting that Jesus did perform many miraculous works or "signs" for the people to see. His signs, however, were not awesome works of magic but demonstrations of his Father's compassion for the suffering and needy, his desire to save us from sin and death. Nevertheless, Jesus was rejected by so many, and still is, precisely because he refused to reduce his ministry to one of working magic tricks.

Jesus was a new Jonah and much more, for he was swallowed by death itself, yet he emerged victorious three days later as the ultimate sign of God's presence and power among us. Now he beckons all people in every age to accept the sign of his cross and come to him. Only then will the mighty work of God's Spirit be released from within the soul and move outward, transforming each of us into another sign of God's action on earth.

"Lord, you are the sign guiding us to the Father. Transform us by your Spirit to become your people, a sign of your covenant of love and mercy."

Luke 11:33-36

33 "No one after lighting a lamp puts it in a cellar or under a
bushel, but on a stand, that those who enter may see the light.
34 Your eye is the lamp of your body; when your eye is sound,
your whole body is full of light, but when it is not sound, your
body is full of darkness. 35 Therefore be careful lest the light in
you be darkness. 36 If then your whole body is full of light,
having no part dark, it will be wholly bright, as when a lamp
with its rays gives you light."

The scientifically accurate description of light is photons that travel through space. No one would claim that Jesus had in mind such a formal definition when he urged us to be like light to the world. Clearly, Jesus wants us to bring the brilliance of God's truth and life to the situations we encounter each day. We understand what Jesus is calling us to do through this passage, but we need to go further and ask him how we are to go about it.

One approach is to muster all the sincerity, determination, and courage we can and then go and try our hardest to be useful and virtuous. Unfortunately, by our own goodness, we can accomplish little of permanent value. Too many good-hearted Christians who want to follow Jesus try to do it on their own power—and they fail. This plays right into Satan's hands; he wants us to try, to see how hard it is, and to fail. Ultimately then, he hopes, we will conclude that it is impossible and stop trying. Jesus' words should lead us to say: "Yes, I want to be a lamp to the world, but how?"

Paul offered the answer to this question which perplexed him as well: "I decided to know nothing among you except Jesus Christ and him crucified . . . that your faith might not rest in the wisdom of men but in the power of God" (1 Corinthians 2:2-5). Paul insisted everywhere that men and women must rely on the power of the triune God to live the Christian life. We must turn to Jesus constantly and rely on him to instruct us, teach us, strengthen us, and enable us to be light to the world.

Let us turn to the great God of all and rely on him. Let us pray, examine our consciences, and repent. Let us read the scriptures for wisdom and participate in the life of the church. In doing these things we will come to know God and to rely on him. Then we will truly be lights to the world.

Luke 11:37-41

37 While he was speaking, a Pharisee asked him to dine with him;
so he went in and sat at table. 38 The Pharisee was astonished to
see that he did not first wash before dinner. 39 And the Lord said
to him, "Now you Pharisees cleanse the outside of the cup and of
the dish, but inside you are full of extortion and wickedness.
40 You fools! Did not he who made the outside make the inside
also? 41 But give for alms those things which are within; and
behold, everything is clean for you.

Give for alms those things which are within, and behold, everything is clean for you. (Luke 11:41)

It may surprise us that Jesus accepted the Pharisee's dinner invitation. They seemed always to be in opposition to one another; disagreements and arguments were a regular part of their interaction. Why would Jesus accept an invitation to spend time with someone who probably disagreed with many of the things that he was saying and doing?

Jesus accepted the Pharisee's invitation—and other similar invitations—in order to demonstrate the Father's priority of giving over observing. Jesus did not have dinner with this Pharisee so that he could observe the things in the Pharisee's life that were against God's will, and then point them out to him. Instead, he decided to give the Pharisee his time and attention and look for an opportunity to share the gospel with him.

The Pharisee, on the other hand, carefully observed Jesus to see if he met all the requirements of the law. Seeing that Jesus failed to wash before the meal (in accordance with strict ritual requirements), he "was astonished" (Luke 11:38). By focusing his attention on Jesus' apparent failures, he elevated himself to the position of judge—a position that belongs to God alone.

Many of the Pharisees placed great importance on obeying a complex system of religious practices, some of which went far beyond the demands of the law of Moses. In contrast, God places importance on two simple laws: Being generous in our love for him and in our love for one another. It can be very challenging for us to give our time, money, attention, or possessions to help others. Such generosity can only come from a heart that is open to God, whose generosity is not only far greater than ours, but is also contagious. Nothing demonstrates the Father's generosity more graphically than the gift of his Son who in his turn gave up his life to rescue us from sin. Let us ask him for the grace to become like him.

"Father, we thank you that you have given us so much. Teach us more about what you have given us in your Son so that in our gratitude we would respond to the work of the Holy Spirit within us and give our lives to help others."

Luke 11:42-46

42 "But woe to you Pharisees! for you tithe mint and rue and
every herb, and neglect justice and the love of God; these you
ought to have done, without neglecting the others. 43 Woe to you
Pharisees! for you love the best seat in the synagogues and
salutations in the market places. 44 Woe to you! for you are like
graves which are not seen, and men walk over them without
knowing it."
45 One of the lawyers answered him, "Teacher, in saying this
you reproach us also." 46 And he said, "Woe to you lawyers also!
for you load men with burdens hard to bear, and you yourselves
do not touch the burdens with one of your fingers.

When he condemned the Pharisees for tithing "mint and rue and every herb" and neglecting "justice and the love of God" (Luke 11:42), Jesus was bringing a fundamental truth into focus. It is not obedience to the letter of the law, but the heart of the law that is most pleasing to God. How easy it can be to overlook this important distinction even today! How easy it is to do things out of habit instead of love for the Lord. And, as a result, how little joy we experience when our religious and moral observances flow from legalism or routine.

In their desire to do all the right things, the Pharisees whom Jesus was addressing had turned their attention toward themselves and their observances. They sought to build up an image of righteousness before others—and before God—that was based on such small issues as whether they had given the right amount of the most insignificant herbs. Given such a situation, what could develop among them except a form of spiritual pride? All the time that they sought to demonstrate their obedience to laws and rituals, they were cutting themselves off from God and storing up judgment for themselves. Even worse, their example kept others from coming to know God personally.

The two greatest commandments show what God desires: to love him with all of our being, and to love our neighbor as ourselves. Both commands demonstrate God's heart and his plan for us. More than anything else, God wants us to have a living relationship with him. As we draw near to him and ask him to imprint his character upon us, he will give us the wisdom to know how to obey him.

God can move us and raise our hearts. We all yearn to love God and to know him as our Father. Have you ever noticed how your heart burns when the Lord reveals to you something of who he is? Let us open our lives to the Lord, and live no longer to satisfy laws, but to take on the character of Jesus our Savior.

"Heavenly Father, fill us with your Spirit and increase in our hearts a desire for your will. You know we are weak, but your heart is merciful. Open our hearts that we would no longer live merely to satisfy a law, but to glorify your name."

Luke 11:47-54

47 Woe to you! for you build the tombs of the prophets whom
your fathers killed. 48 So you are witnesses and consent to the
deeds of your fathers; for they killed them, and you build their
tombs. 49 Therefore also the Wisdom of God said, 'I will send
them prophets and apostles, some of whom they will kill and
persecute,' 50 that the blood of all the prophets, shed from the
foundation of the world, may be required of this generation,
51 from the blood of Abel to the blood of Zechariah, who
perished between the altar and the sanctuary. Yes, I tell you, it
shall be required of this generation. 52 Woe to you lawyers! for
you have taken away the key of knowledge; you did not enter
yourselves, and you hindered those who were entering."
53 As he went away from there, the scribes and the Pharisees
began to press him hard, and to provoke him to speak of many
things, 54 lying in wait for him, to catch at something he
might say.

Jesus loved the Pharisees, even though they appeared to be enemies. His mission was to draw all people to himself, and this was his desire for these men as well. Jesus' love for the inspired word of God, and his love for God's people who were being misled by the distortions of the Pharisees, caused him to denounce and speak out strongly against them.

The Pharisees were little different than their ancestors. Jesus used the example of the rejection of the prophets as an illustration of the Pharisees' hypocrisy and blindness. From Abel to Zechariah (who was murdered in the temple as he tried to call the nation back to true worship), the leaders of the people had closed their minds to the word of God and replaced it with their own ideas.

While appearing to be religious, they had tried to make religion serve them and their desires, rather than allowing religion to move them to hear God and respond to him in obedience.

The Wisdom of God was in their midst, yet they could not see the Lord. They sought to destroy Jesus rather than embrace his teaching and example. The Pharisees had taken away the "key of knowledge" (Luke 11:52), and in the process failed to gain entrance to the house of wisdom and prevented others from entering as well. Jesus is the "door" (John 10:7)—the entrance to all wisdom and knowledge of God. By rejecting him, the Pharisees rejected wisdom and knowledge of God, and thus they closed themselves to the work God wanted to do in transforming them.

Through his prophets, God prepared the way for salvation by the death of his own Son. The leaders consistently rejected the word of the prophets. We face similar choices in our own lives. God wants to teach us every day through Jesus. Will we choose to follow him, or will we choose to interpret the scriptures and commands of God to suit our own desires? Will we choose to follow Jesus and let his new life reign in us, or will we let our old angers and greed rule us? These are the choices we face.

"Loving Father, may your Spirit lead me to Jesus. Through him, may I be brought to the house of wisdom and be transformed. Let me choose life and live!"

The Kingdom Meets with Opposition

Luke
12–14

Luke 12:1-7

1 In the meantime, when so many thousands of the multitude
had gathered together that they trod upon one another, he began
to say to his disciples first, "Beware of the leaven of the
Pharisees, which is hypocrisy. 2 Nothing is covered up that will
not be revealed, or hidden that will not be known. 3 Whatever
you have said in the dark shall be heard in the light, and what
you have whispered in private rooms shall be proclaimed upon
the housetops.
4 "I tell you, my friends, do not fear those who kill the body,
and after that have no more that they can do. 5 But I will warn
you whom to fear: fear him who, after he has killed, has power to
cast into hell; yes, I tell you, fear him! 6 Are not five sparrows
sold for two pennies? And not one of them is forgotten before
God. 7 Why, even the hairs of your head are all numbered. Fear
not; you are of more value than many sparrows."

How seemingly contradictory! First, Jesus told his disciples to fear, then that there is no need to be afraid (Luke 12:5,7). In fact, Jesus was teaching his disciples what to fear and what not to fear. On the one hand, we are to "fear God," in the sense of being in awe of who he is. In its deepest reality, this means recognizing the profound difference between us and God. On the other hand, this same awesome God (whom we are to fear) should hold no terror for us, because, as Jesus said: "Take heart, it is I; have no fear" (Matthew 14:27).

Human fear makes us anxious and upset. It is crucial, therefore, that we experience the unchanging and boundless love that God has for us. This love is not abstract; it is personal, intimate, compassionate. Indeed, with gentle incongruity, Jesus reminds us of the care the Father exercises for sparrows (Luke 12:6), that were sold as a cheap source of food. How much more does he care for those who are created in his image, those destined to be his adopted children!

Sin makes us timid and self-conscious before God. We tend to cringe before him like the man who buried his one talent because he feared his master (see Matthew 25:24-25). As long as we think of God as someone who does not care about our well-being, we will remain afraid. Faced with life's uncertainties—with sickness, loneliness, and personal misfortune—we need to rouse our faith by recalling that God wants only the best for us.

There is nothing in us that can merit the love of a just and holy God, yet we have God's own word that nothing in the whole universe can stop him from loving us (see Romans 8:31-39). Jesus' death and resurrection show that God's love is stronger than our fear of death (see Hebrews 2:14-15). Our security, therefore, is not in what we are, but in what God has declared himself to be.

As long as we trust ourselves to the whims of chance or to the world, as long as we are willing to live by our own standards of goodness, we will find ourselves at the mercy of fear. But as we commit our lives to a loving Jesus who constantly beckons us to his embrace, we will come to know both his perfect love and that "perfect love casts out fear" (1 John 4:18).

Luke 12:8-12

8 "And I tell you, every one who acknowledges me before
men, the Son of man also will acknowledge before the angels of
God; 9 but he who denies me before men will be denied before

the angels of God. [10] And every one who speaks a word against
the Son of man will be forgiven; but he who blasphemes against
the Holy Spirit will not be forgiven. [11] And when they bring you
before the synagogues and the rulers and the authorities, do not
be anxious how or what you are to answer or what you are to say;
[12] for the Holy Spirit will teach you in that very hour what you
ought to say."

With great confidence, Jesus entrusted his disciples to the care of the Holy Spirit. This Spirit, whose goal is to lead believers into all truth (see John 16:13) and remind them of Jesus' words (see John 14:26), would be with them when they faced hostile forces in the world (see Luke 12:11). This Spirit, who is promised to all who believe and are baptized (see Acts 2:38-39), would be their one source of strength, wisdom and consolation as they sought to follow Jesus and become more and more like him. For these reasons Jesus warned against blaspheming against the Spirit (see Luke 12:10).

To deny God's desire to dwell within us and make us like him is to deny that he has the power to do such wonderful things. To slip into fear or confusion is to believe tacitly that the Spirit isn't sufficient to answer our prayers or strengthen us in difficulties. Similarly, to move through our days as if we had the answers to all our needs is to say that the Spirit isn't God's life given to a needy people, but only an "extra," a nice optional gift from God, but not the true source of life.

Luke presented his readers with stories and teachings about the opposition—internal and external—that believers can expect. Each type of opposition is sufficient in and of itself to overwhelm or drain from a disciple the joy of following Jesus. Yet Jesus' words remain true: The disciple is never alone. Through the indwelling

Spirit, believers have unending access to the throne of grace. Though the flesh can rage and the devil taunt, the heart of every Christian can remain steadfast and trusting.

Jesus told his disciples: "Fear not, little flock, for it is your Father's good pleasure to give you the kingdom" (Luke 12:32). The kingdom of God is present wherever the Spirit has freedom to work. Today, let us hold fast in our hearts to the fact that the Spirit has been given to transform us; the Spirit is in the church to sanctify its members; and the Spirit is in the world to bring redemption to all who turn to Christ.

"Come, Holy Spirit, fill the hearts of your faithful and kindle in them the fire of your love. Send forth your Spirit, and they shall be created; and you shall renew the face of the earth."

Luke 12:13-21

13 One of the multitude said to him, "Teacher, bid my brother
divide the inheritance with me." 14 But he said to him, "Man,
who made me a judge or divider over you?" 15 And he said to
them, "Take heed, and beware of all covetousness; for a man's life
does not consist in the abundance of his possessions." 16 And he
told them a parable, saying, "The land of a rich man brought
forth plentifully; 17 and he thought to himself, 'What shall I do,
for I have nowhere to store my crops?' 18 And he said, 'I will do
this: I will pull down my barns, and build larger ones; and there I
will store all my grain and my goods. 19 And I will say to my soul,
Soul, you have ample goods laid up for many years; take your
ease, eat, drink, be merry.' 20 But God said to him, 'Fool! This
night your soul is required of you; and the things you have
prepared, whose will they be?' 21 So is he who lays up treasure for
himself, and is not rich toward God."

What would you do if you suddenly inherited a large sum of money? Would you buy a vacation home or a new car? Would you quit your job and retire? Would you view your inheritance as all your own, to use however you liked, or would you see it as a gift from God, who might have other plans for how the money should be spent?

The man in the parable saw his unexpected wealth as his due, and he made plans to keep hold of it as long as he could. Jesus showed us that the man was deluding himself. Not only was this "bumper crop" a gift from God, so too was the man's life. Without the gift of life, the man's wealth became utterly useless.

Jesus indicates that anyone "who lays up treasure for himself, and is not rich toward God" is foolish (Luke 12:21). What does it mean to be "rich toward God"? When we view our possessions, and even our very lives, as a pure and undeserved gift from God, we are much better disposed to be generous to others. Jesus "died for all, that those who live might live no longer for themselves but for him who for their sake died and was raised" (2 Corinthians 5:15). As we come to understand that we have received such a wonderful gift, we will naturally be compelled to reflect Jesus' graciousness towards others.

Mother Teresa is probably one of this century's greatest examples of one compelled to radical generosity by Jesus' love. Her words can also inspire us to greater generosity:

> Open your hearts to the love God instills in them. God loves you tenderly. What he gives you is not to be kept under lock and key, but to be shared. The more you save, the less you will be able to give. The less you have, the more you will know how to share. Let us ask God, when it comes time to ask him for something, to help us to be generous. (*Mother Teresa, In Her Own Words*, p. 18)

"Lord Jesus, help us to see that our Father in heaven is the true source of all our possessions. Give us the grace to share everything you have given us with those who have less. In this way, may we become generous toward you."

Luke 12:22-31

22 And he said to his disciples, "Therefore I tell you, do not be
anxious about your life, what you shall eat, nor about your body,
what you shall put on. 23 For life is more than food, and the
body more than clothing. 24 Consider the ravens: they neither
sow nor reap, they have neither storehouse nor barn, and yet
God feeds them. Of how much more value are you than the
birds! 25 And which of you by being anxious can add a cubit to
his span of life? 26 If then you are not able to do as small a thing
as that, why are you anxious about the rest? 27 Consider the
lilies, how they grow; they neither toil nor spin; yet I tell you,
even Solomon in all his glory was not arrayed like one of these.
28 But if God so clothes the grass which is alive in the field today
and tomorrow is thrown into the oven, how much more will he
clothe you, O men of little faith! 29 And do not seek what you
are to eat and what you are to drink, nor be of anxious mind.
30 For all the nations of the world seek these things, and your
Father knows that you need them. 31 Instead, seek his kingdom,
and these things shall be yours as well."

The world we live in is very materialistic, very pragmatic, and very self-reliant. We find that every day we must devote great amounts of our time and energy to making proper provision for the necessities of our lives. Because of this way of thinking and acting, we may feel that it is impossible to be obedient to the exhortation to live in trust that God will provide for our needs. And so we pass over it with feelings of inadequacy.

This happens because we fail to grasp the most important verse in the passage: "Seek his kingdom" (Luke 12:31). Before we can ever begin to live free of our bondage to worldly desires, we must learn to seek the kingdom of God, to live the spiritual life.

Central to the Christian life is our acceptance of the truth that Jesus Christ is the Lord of the universe. Every day we must reassert our belief in this and strive to live in obedience to Christ. Without the divine power that comes from the Holy Spirit, it is a completely impossible task. As we pray and read scripture daily, the Spirit will begin to direct our minds, revealing to us the gospel truths and our total dependence upon Christ for life.

The life of sin and material gain can be quite appealing, making the spiritual life seem even more difficult and unattractive. The deception and emptiness of the sinful life are revealed to us by the Holy Spirit as he prepares us to fight the battle in our minds. We learn that our sins are forgiven, that we can be made alive in Christ, that we can have power over our sin and know the hope of eternal life in heaven.

If we beg the Spirit to direct us daily, if we are faithful to prayer and the scriptures, our minds will be transformed. Our "pragmatic" ways of thinking will be balanced by a concern for our spiritual welfare and the state of our families. We will find that our needs will be met. Besides that, we will still have the energy and the desire to think about the Lord and worship him for his saving death and resurrection. In short, we will gain access to the mind of Christ (see 1 Corinthians 2:16).

Luke 12:32-34

32 "Fear not, little flock, for it is your Father's good pleasure to
give you the kingdom. 33 Sell your possessions, and give alms;
provide yourselves with purses that do not grow old, with a
treasure in the heavens that does not fail, where no thief
approaches and no moth destroys. 34 For where your treasure is,
there will your heart be also."

Jesus' exhortation to store up treasure in heaven makes it clear that there are two ways of doing these things: One is designed to win the admiration of people; the other is intended to please God.

What is the difference between actions which produce permanent treasure in heaven and the same deeds done in a way that achieves only temporary results on earth? It is not just a matter of one being done in private and the other taking place before the eyes of the world; the difference lies in the attitude of the heart.

One is more interested in serving God and fellow human beings than in performing a ritual. When people act from motivations of pure love, they do not care if anyone knows about their deeds. Their only concern is that the actions achieve the ends for which they were taken. They forget both the cost to themselves and likelihood of getting credit.

St. Augustine spoke about this in one of his sermons: "If the heart be on earth, that is, if one perform anything with a heart bent on obtaining earthly advantage, how will that heart be clean which wallows on earth? But if it be in heaven, it will be clean, because whatever things are heavenly are clean. For anything becomes polluted when it is mixed with a nature that is inferior . . . for gold is polluted even by pure silver, if it is mixed with it: so also our mind becomes polluted by the desire of earthly things. . . . All our works are pure and well-pleasing in the sight of God, when they are done with a single heart, that is, with a heavenly intent, having the end of love in view; for love is also the fulfilling of the law."

Let us ask God to give us the love to serve him alone. "Father, forgive us for seeking to impress others with our service which ought to be done for love of you alone. Create in us pure hearts which will enable us to love you and please you."

Luke 12:35-38

35 "Let your loins be girded and your lamps burning, 36 and be
like men who are waiting for their master to come home from
the marriage feast, so that they may open to him at once when
he comes and knocks. 37 Blessed are those servants whom the
master finds awake when he comes; truly, I say to you, he will
gird himself and have them sit at table, and he will come and
serve them. 38 If he comes in the second watch, or in the third,
and finds them so, blessed are those servants!"

In anticipation of their master's return from his wedding feast, the servants had dressed in proper attire, prepared food, cleaned the house, lit lamps so that he and his new bride could easily find their way to the door, and stationed themselves so that they could immediately respond to their needs. It was very late, and they were tired, but none of them fell asleep or shirked their duties. Finally, their master knocked! Eager to care for him and his wife, they immediately opened the door and welcomed them. Imagine their surprise when their master invited them to sit down and then went about the business of tending to their needs and serving them refreshments!

How blessed those servants would feel! Their master had treated them with love and compassion, enabling them to love him in return. What is this parable, but an indication of our lives as servants of the great Master, Jesus? He has called each of us to serve him in preparation for the day when he is united with his bride, the church—and to share in his abundant joy on that day.

As servants, will we indulge ourselves in our Master's absence, or will we stand alert, ready to do his bidding? Jesus is eager to reward those who have labored in his absence and are awake and ready when he returns. He is a loving redeemer and protector unlike any earthly master we will ever know. King though he was, Jesus performed the ultimate act of service for his followers: He laid down his life on the cross so that we could be united with him forever.

Our Master's return will be a glorious day for those who believe in him and have sought to know him through prayer and the scriptures. On that day, he will acknowledge how hard we have worked for him and shower us with love in return. He will embrace his faithful servants, saying: "Come, refresh your souls, partake in my wedding feast, and share in my joy. Sit down and I will wash the dirt of earthly trials, suffering, and hardship from your feet, anoint you with costly oil, and clothe you in heavenly garments."

"Lord, help us to serve you faithfully so that on the last day, we may receive the greatest of rewards—the fullness of joy in your presence."

Luke 12:39-48

39 But know this, that if the householder had known at what
hour the thief was coming, he would have been awake and would
not have left his house to be broken into. 40 You also must be
ready; for the Son of man is coming at an hour you do not
expect." 41 Peter said, "Lord, are you telling this parable for us or
for all?" 42 And the Lord said, "Who then is the faithful and wise
steward, whom his master will set over his household, to give
them their portion of food at the proper time? 43 Blessed is that
servant whom his master when he comes will find so doing.
44 Truly, I tell you, he will set him over all his possessions. 45 But
if that servant says to himself, 'My master is delayed in coming,'
and begins to beat the menservants and the maidservants, and to
eat and drink and get drunk, 46 the master of that servant will
come on a day when he does not expect him and at an hour he
does not know, and will punish him, and put him with the
unfaithful. 47 And that servant who knew his master's will, but
did not make ready or act according to his will, shall receive a
severe beating. 48 But he who did not know, and did what
deserved a beating, shall receive a light beating. Every one to
whom much is given, of him will much be required; and of him
to whom men commit much they will demand the more.

Peter asked Jesus whether his teaching about dedicated service was intended for the twelve disciples only, or for all his followers (Luke 12:41). Jesus' answer was general enough to allow for both possibilities; no one is excluded from the call to serve Christ with complete attention and watchfulness.

The Greek word for "servant" is *doulos* (Luke 12:43,45-47) and can be translated as either "servant" or "slave." A *doulos* in Jesus' time was more a slave than a hired servant. The word implied a total ownership on the part of the master and called for complete obedience to the master's will. A slave's service was unconditional and his complete devotion to the master was taken for granted.

By using this word, Luke was describing the service to which God calls us. In all circumstances—in our parishes, in our relationships at work, in our families or other groups—God wants us to contribute our time, energy, and knowledge in a selfless way. He calls us to serve without complaint or reservation, lovingly, looking beyond our own comfort to the needs of others and the concerns of the church. Jesus said: "Every one to whom much is given, of him will much be required" (Luke 12:48). We have been baptized into the riches of Christ, into a bountiful inheritance, but one which is not intended just for our security and comfort. Jesus has given everything to us so that we might share with others what we have received.

Ordinarily, we might think that this level of service is too hard, that too much is being asked of us. Who would ever want such a commission? This is where Jesus totally transformed the concept of service: He called people to give themselves to him unconditionally, to belong to him as his people and his servants, living for the desires of their master.

Service to Christ is not one-sided, however. Jesus graciously showers us with a knowledge of his love and salvation as we give of ourselves. He does not insist that we work to exhaustion, but that we consecrate our lives, just as he did. He has promised us that if we renounce our self-directed ways and shoulder the yoke of his service, we will experience a fullness of life and peace which we could never achieve on our own.

Luke 12:49-53

49 "I came to cast fire upon the earth; and would that it were
already kindled! 50 I have a baptism to be baptized with; and
how I am constrained until it is accomplished! 51 Do you think
that I have come to give peace on earth? No, I tell you, but
rather division; 52 for henceforth in one house there will be five
divided, three against two and two against three; 53 they will be
divided, father against son and son against father, mother
against daughter and daughter against her mother, mother-in-
law against her daughter-in-law and daughter-in-law against her
mother-in-law."

Fire and division—two powerful images packed into one brief passage of scripture. Sometimes, it can be difficult not to question God's compassion when he speaks to us through such dark images! Our Father clearly has an abundance of peace and unity to bring into our lives, but even as we stand firm in our faith, there are times when we may encounter strife and disagreement—even within our own families.

Jesus told his disciples to seek first the kingdom of God, and that "the rest" would follow (see Matthew 6:33). But "the rest" is not always a life without difficulty. Given the state of our world, it is unrealistic to expect a totally carefree existence. What is it, then, that will surely follow? It is the promises made in Hebrews 12—a life of discipline and grace in Christ. No matter what our situation, we can trust that Jesus is always with us, helping us to work through the difficulties we face in this world.

When he spoke of the fire that he wished were already kindled, Jesus was talking of the Holy Spirit who was to come after him to fill every heart. The divisions he spoke of referred to people or ideologies opposing God, and how that which opposes God will be separated from his kingdom. This message of faith challenges people and their relationships, even the strongest bonds of love found in our families.

In the face of these challenges, how should we respond to those who may not agree with the word of God? We should never be reluctant to speak of the gospel's truths. God will protect us as we stand up for the gospel. We are called to be unafraid of his purifying fire. Let us eagerly embrace his word as well as the dividing sword of the Holy Spirit as it moves swiftly to separate "wheat from chaff" (Luke 3:17).

"Lord Jesus, we dedicate ourselves to you right now. No matter what the cost, we want to follow your way, not the way of this world."

Luke 12:54-59

54 He also said to the multitudes, "When you see a cloud rising
in the west, you say at once, 'A shower is coming'; and so it
happens. 55 And when you see the south wind blowing, you say,
'There will be scorching heat'; and it happens. 56 You hypocrites!
You know how to interpret the appearance of earth and sky; but
why do you not know how to interpret the present time?
57 "And why do you not judge for yourselves what is right?
58 As you go with your accuser before the magistrate, make an
effort to settle with him on the way, lest he drag you to the
judge, and the judge hand you over to the officer, and the officer
put you in prison. 59 I tell you, you will never get out till you
have paid the very last copper."

In some ways, those in the crowd knew how to understand and respond to the course of events around them. Clouds spell rain; a southerly wind means heat. It's not hard in either situation to know how to dress or plan your activities. The people were willing to respond intelligently to the natural events in their lives, but unwilling to respond to supernatural events, some of which were far more clear and dependable than weather forecasts.

Jesus asked why they could not understand the "present time" as accurately as they could understand the weather or the necessities of legal action (Luke 12:56). The Greek word for "time" here is *kairon*, and in the New Testament it frequently refers to a specific time appointed by God. The signs of the times were all around them: Loaves being multiplied, the lame walking, hardened sinners repenting, and the good news spreading. Jesus himself stood among them as a manifestation of his Father's love and power. How could anyone surrounded by such signs not be compelled to examine his openness to seeing the work of God?

Today, no less than in ancient Palestine, the signs are around us. The entire world has been transformed by the resurrection of Christ and the outpouring of the Holy Spirit, and the signs are there if we would but open our eyes. We see these signs in miracles, healings, restored relationships, Christian joy, and fellowship with other believers. We see them too through people who respond to God's grace and mediate his love to the suffering in our parishes, soup kitchens, and clinics both at home and abroad. These are but a few of the things we will see. So much evidence is available if we take time to look and listen for the work of God in our midst.

Jesus urges his listeners to read these signs and act while there still is time to do so (Luke 12:57-59). The parable about going to court to settle differences points to God and his judgment. Dealing justly with one's neighbor is the proper response God calls for, and doing so prepares us for the coming judgment.

"Heavenly Father, in your mercy you have redeemed us and opened heaven for us. By your Spirit, help us recognize the signs of your love and power. Show us how to respond to your gracious invitation to life."

Luke 13:1-9

1 There were some present at that very time who told him of
the Galileans whose blood Pilate had mingled with their
sacrifices. 2 And he answered them, "Do you think that these
Galileans were worse sinners than all the other Galileans,
because they suffered thus? 3 I tell you, No; but unless you
repent you will all likewise perish. 4 Or those eighteen upon
whom the tower in Siloam fell and killed them, do you think
that they were worse offenders than all the others who dwelt in
Jerusalem? 5 I tell you, No; but unless you repent you will all
likewise perish."
6 And he told this parable: "A man had a fig tree planted in
his vineyard; and he came seeking fruit on it and found none.
7 And he said to the vinedresser, 'Lo, these three years I have
come seeking fruit on this fig tree, and I find none. Cut it down;
why should it use up the ground?' 8 And he answered him, 'Let
it alone, sir, this year also, till I dig about it and put on manure.
9 And if it bears fruit next year, well and good; but if not, you
can cut it down.' "

In his unending patience, God gives his people numerous opportunities to turn to him in repentance and bear the fruit of his life within them. He never tires of welcoming us back to him. He sees our potential to bear fruit and will help us if we but repent. But, as Jesus' parable illustrates, this is no excuse for delaying our response.

If we were "in charge," we would probably be much quicker than Jesus to condemn those committing sins, especially sins that hurt us directly. How many times have we wished that a particularly unpleasant person would receive his or her due? However, if we treat others according to the demands of retribution, we would have to submit ourselves to the same form of justice—not a pleasant prospect. Sinners ourselves, we too would stand condemned.

Thankfully, God doesn't work that way. While he knows that we deserve condemnation, he withholds judgment in the hope that we will accept his call. God is not the author of retribution and misfortune, and he does not rejoice in the destruction of the wicked (see Ezekiel 18:32). He offers only goodness and life. The prayer of the psalmist rings out: "Bless the Lord . . . who forgives . . . who heals . . . who redeems . . . who crowns you with steadfast love and mercy" (Psalm 103:2-4).

If God treats us with mercy and love, how should we treat others? Our willingness to serve others is a reliable measure of how fully we have embraced the love and mercy of our Father. Far from despairing of humankind, he sent his own Son to preach conversion and fill us with his Spirit. Let us reach out to others with the same patience and love we have received from God. Let us also ask the Spirit to increase our ability to receive mercy and grace from him.

"Lord Jesus, we come to you with grateful hearts, for you provide the way back to our heavenly Father. Help us yield to your Spirit as we reach out to others."

Luke 13:10-17

10 Now he was teaching in one of the synagogues on the
sabbath. 11 And there was a woman who had had a spirit of
infirmity for eighteen years; she was bent over and could not
fully straighten herself. 12 And when Jesus saw her, he called her
and said to her, "Woman, you are freed from your infirmity."
13 And he laid his hands upon her, and immediately she was
made straight, and she praised God. 14 But the ruler of the
synagogue, indignant because Jesus had healed on the sabbath,
said to the people, "There are six days on which work ought to
be done; come on those days and be healed, and not on the
sabbath day." 15 Then the Lord answered him, "You hypocrites!
Does not each of you on the sabbath untie his ox or his ass from
the manger, and lead it away to water it? 16 And ought not this
woman, a daughter of Abraham whom Satan bound for eighteen
years, be loosed from this bond on the sabbath day?" 17 As he
said this, all his adversaries were put to shame; and all the people
rejoiced at all the glorious things that were done by him.

An encounter with Jesus always brings great healing and dignity. That is because Jesus does not see us as we see ourselves or as others see us. In his eyes, we all have great value because we are beloved of God and made in his image. The woman whom Jesus healed had been so stripped of her dignity that she was considered less important than a thirsty barnyard animal. At least they could be cared for on the Sabbath! But Jesus saw this woman differently. He called her a "daughter of Abraham" (Luke 13:16), a member of God's chosen people, and he healed her so that she could once more stand as a woman of dignity, no longer burdened by Satan.

Society places such importance on externals, on doing certain things certain ways. The synagogue ruler thought little of this "daughter of Abraham" and little of Jesus. Blinded by his hypocrisy, he could not see what was happening before his very eyes. The kingdom of God had come with great power, calling him to the freedom of being a son of God. But he missed it because of his narrow view of how God would work. God would only heal during the "working week," not on the official day of rest.

Perhaps our experience is like the woman's. We may be deeply burdened by Satan. We may feel stripped of our dignity through painful experiences or debilitating illness. Perhaps we are like the synagogue ruler, blinded by commands and duties and unable to perceive the priority of love. We may have become harsh and judgmental to the point that we don't see how valuable we—and others—really are in God's eyes.

Let us not feel so sure of how God will work that we don't give him the freedom to work outside of the boundary lines we have set up for him. Jesus can set us free of anything that binds or oppresses us. Let us turn to him now so that he can restore to us the dignity that each of us has as beloved sons and daughters of God.

"Lord Jesus, heal us of our illnesses, burdens, and wounds. Set us free from the power of Satan and fill us with love for you so that, like this 'daughter of Abraham,' we too might praise you for the dignity you have given us."

Luke 13:18-21

18 He said therefore, "What is the kingdom of God like? And
to what shall I compare it? 19 It is like a grain of mustard seed
which a man took and sowed in his garden; and it grew and
became a tree, and the birds of the air made nests in its branches."

20 And again he said, "To what shall I compare the kingdom of God? 21 It is like leaven which a woman took and hid in three measures of meal, till it was all leavened."

It's a fallacy to think that God's work in our lives must begin like a clap of thunder or a bolt of lightning. More often than not, his work begins with something small, perhaps even mundane. Mother Teresa of Calcutta often told the story of how she came to pick up the first destitute, dying person from the street: "If I had not picked up that first man, I would not have picked up the thousands since then."

St. Francis de Sales (1567-1622) was another who spoke of the value of allowing God to change our behavior in small things: "Great opportunities to serve God rarely present themselves," he wrote, "but little ones are frequent. Whoever will be 'faithful over a few things,' will be placed 'over many,' says the Savior."

St. Francis de Sales commended the example of another great saint: "When I saw in St. Catherine of Siena's life so many raptures and elevations of spirit, words of wisdom, and even sermons uttered by her, I did not doubt that by the eye of contemplation she had ravished the heart of her heavenly Spouse. But I was equally comforted when I saw her in her father's kitchen, humbly turning the spit, kindling fires, dressing meat, kneading bread, and doing the meanest household chores cheerfully and filled with love and affection for God" (*Introduction to the Devout Life*, Part III, 35).

It is easy to be blind to the prosaic ways God wants to work in our lives—to heal the way we speak to members of our families or treat those with whom we work. Let us resolve to be obedient to the daily promptings of the Holy Spirit to turn away from sin, to accept forgiveness when we fall, to readily forgive all who hurt us, and to spend time with the Lord in daily prayer and scripture reading. Then we may be confident that the kingdom of God will daily grow in our lives as a mustard seed becomes a great shrub or as yeast produces abundant bread.

"Lord, open my eyes to the ways you would work in my life this very day. I pray that your kingdom would come and benefit all whom you desire to touch and save through my life. Let me know your love that I might allow you to work through me."

Luke 13:22-30

22 He went on his way through towns and villages, teaching,
and journeying toward Jerusalem. 23 And some one said to him,
"Lord, will those who are saved be few?" And he said to them,
24 "Strive to enter by the narrow door; for many, I tell you, will
seek to enter and will not be able. 25 When once the householder
has risen up and shut the door, you will begin to stand outside
and to knock at the door, saying, 'Lord, open to us.' He will
answer you, 'I do not know where you come from.' 26 Then you
will begin to say, 'We ate and drank in your presence, and you
taught in our streets.' 27 But he will say, 'I tell you, I do not know
where you come from; depart from me, all you workers of
iniquity!' 28 There you will weep and gnash your teeth, when you
see Abraham and Isaac and Jacob and all the prophets in the
kingdom of God and you yourselves thrust out. 29 And men will
come from east and west, and from north and south, and sit at
table in the kingdom of God. 30 And behold, some are last who
will be first, and some are first who will be last."

Jesus never beat around the bush when he described the judgment that all of us will face at the end of our lives. He used vivid parables to help us understand and prepare for it. When we read about the closing of the "narrow door" on the day of judgment, it's easy to imagine the horror a person would feel on hearing Christ say: "Depart from me, all you workers of iniquity" (Luke 13:27). Jesus said that some people would actually hear this dreadful sentence pronounced and be surprised by it because they will be people who are acquainted with him and his teachings (13:26).

While Jesus did not sugar-coat the gospel, neither did his words foretell dire consequences for all—only for those who ignore his instruction. Those who take it to heart will experience his salvation. "Therefore we must pay the closer attention to what we have heard, lest we drift away from it" (Hebrews 2:1). Our response should be the same as that of Peter's listeners on that first Pentecost: "Now when they heard this they were cut to the heart, and said . . . 'Brethren, what shall we do?' " (Acts 2:37).

First we ought to be certain in our hearts that we have indeed "entered through the narrow door." Without allowing our own sense of self-esteem to cloud our analysis, we need to ask the Holy Spirit to show us our true condition before God. Once we have acknowledged the depth of our sin and our need for Jesus, we can put our hope in Christ, for "God sent the Son into the world, not to condemn the world, but that the world might be saved through him" (John 3:17).

Having entered through the narrow door of faith in Christ, we are safe in God's stronghold. "He who believes in him is not condemned" (John 3:18). No longer need we fear the day that the owner of the house will shut the door against us. We are already inside!

Henceforth, our goal will not be to get in, but to stay in. Satan may attack us—with doubts, fears, resentments, discouragement, and accusations. He may try to persuade us that we are still out in the cold. Worldly occupations and pleasures may seek to dull our desire for the life that Jesus offers. We must stand fast in faith! If we abide in Christ, we need never fear. "This is the victory that overcomes the world, our faith" (1 John 5:4).

Luke 13:31-35

31 At that very hour some Pharisees came, and said to him, "Get
away from here, for Herod wants to kill you." 32 And he said to
them, "Go and tell that fox, 'Behold, I cast out demons and
perform cures today and tomorrow, and the third day I finish my
course. 33 Nevertheless I must go on my way today and tomorrow
and the day following; for it cannot be that a prophet should
perish away from Jerusalem.' 34 O Jerusalem, Jerusalem, killing
the prophets and stoning those who are sent to you! How often
would I have gathered your children together as a hen gathers her
brood under her wings, and you would not! 35 Behold, your house
is forsaken. And I tell you, you will not see me until you say,
'Blessed is he who comes in the name of the Lord!' "

Neither Herod, in his desire to kill Jesus, nor the Pharisees, in their attempt to protect him, could dissuade Jesus from fulfilling the Father's plan of salvation. That plan was formed long ago, and Jesus had dedicated his life to carrying it out. He knew that he must meet Jerusalem and the cross, and he said as much to the Pharisees: "I must go on my way . . . for it cannot be that a prophet should perish away from Jerusalem" (Luke 13:33).

As he journeyed to his final hour, Jesus mourned, for he was well aware that his sacrifice of love would not be able to save those who rejected him. Jerusalem had been the scene of the brutal murders of many of God's prophets; Jesus would be no exception. Yet, he wanted the children of Jerusalem to come to him. Just as a mother and father cannot force a wayward child back to them, Jesus could not demand that his people respond to his offer of mercy and redemption.

Jesus' words revealed the heart of one who grieves for us, not for himself. He would go willingly to the cross to win our forgiveness. Without a trace of bitterness or resentment, he freely showed his compassion for all people. As Jesus foretold, he would arrive in Jerusalem amidst cries of praise: "Blessed is the King who comes in the name of the Lord!" (Luke 19:38). Days later, however, he would be crucified. The people who rejoiced at his entrance into Jerusalem would later release a notorious prisoner, rather than save Jesus from the cross (23:18-19). They would forsake Jesus and, by their own choosing, their house would be forsaken. How this knowledge must have saddened Jesus as he mourned over Jerusalem's rejection of him.

Our own "house" need not be forsaken. Though we are sinners, Jesus awaits us, longing to gather us to him. Nothing that we have ever done, however sinful, can keep him from loving us. God never forces us to return to him. As he did with the people of Jerusalem, he respects our freedom, always leaving the decision to us.

"Lord Jesus, thank you for loving us even though we have turned away from you. Help us to come under your loving care. Bring everyone—even those who seem far away from you—into your embrace."

Luke 14:1-6

1 One sabbath when he went to dine at the house of a ruler
who belonged to the Pharisees, they were watching him. 2 And
behold, there was a man before him who had dropsy. 3 And Jesus
spoke to the lawyers and Pharisees, saying, "Is it lawful to heal
on the sabbath, or not?" 4 But they were silent. Then he took
him and healed him, and let him go. 5 And he said to them,
"Which of you, having an ass or an ox that has fallen into a well,
will not immediately pull him out on a sabbath day?" 6 And they
could not reply to this.

Once again, Jesus found himself in the middle of controversy over healing on the sabbath. The Pharisees' limited interpretation of God's commands led them to watch Jesus closely, looking for any opportunity to trip him up. For his part, Jesus took their scrutiny as a chance to teach them about the heart of God's law, which consists of mercy and healing.

When Jesus healed the man with dropsy—an ailment that caused excessive retention of fluid, possibly connected to a heart condition—he once more confronted the Pharisees' narrow understanding of God's ways. Their rigid application of sabbath law left no room for the love and mercy that are the foundation of every one of God's commands. Jesus addressed their rigidity directly, exposing the hypocrisy of their attitude. If any sensible person would rescue a farm animal in mortal danger, how much more would God want to rescue one of his children in need? Of all the days of the week, the Sabbath would be the most appropriate day for God's children to receive his healing touch. He has always wanted us to enter into his rest.

The sabbath rest God wants for us comes from an intimate experience of his love and mercy. It is this intimacy with God that places peace in our hearts, no matter what our circumstances might be. We know God to be a loving and powerful Father, and we know we belong to him. We learn to trust in his provision and we surrender our lives to his care. Jesus came to inaugurate God's sabbath rest on earth through his suffering, death, and resurrection. As his people, the church, we can now experience it in increasing depth.

How do we experience God's rest? The most essential element is prayer, which puts us into contact with the realities of God's kingdom. As we open ourselves to God through prayer, scripture, and the sacramental life of the church, God's life penetrates our beings more fully. As we rest ourselves in Christ through prayer and humble obedience, we become more confident of his love for us, and we receive his healing touch more deeply.

"Lord Jesus, we open our hearts to you now. Let us enter into your rest and experience your mercy and healing. Help us to see that the heart of your law is love."

Luke 14:7-11

7 Now he told a parable to those who were invited, when he
marked how they chose the places of honor, saying to them,
8 "When you are invited by any one to a marriage feast, do not
sit down in a place of honor, lest a more eminent man than you
be invited by him;
9 and he who invited you both will come and
say to you, 'Give place to this man,' and then you will begin
with shame to take the lowest place.
10 But when you are
invited, go and sit in the lowest place, so that when your host
comes he may say to you, 'Friend, go up higher'; then you will be
honored in the presence of all who sit at table with you.
11 For

every one who exalts himself will be humbled, and he who humbles himself will be exalted."

Everyone who exalts himself will be humbled, and he who humbles himself will be exalted. (Luke 14:11)

Jesus spoke these words as he taught the way of discipleship. These words seem straightforward enough. When we look more closely, however, we can hear Jesus speak to us from the heart with love. Jesus learned obedience to the Father. When we find him speaking to the people about attitudes of the heart, we know that he was not reciting some dry doctrine from an elevated level. Rather, he was explaining with compassion what he himself had learned from experience.

Jesus could speak about humility because he had learned to be humble before the Father. He could say, "Give, and it will be given to you. A good measure, pressed down, shaken together, running over, will be put into your lap" (Luke 6:38), because this was his own experience of God the Father's love! While he walked the earth, Jesus gave all he had by embracing the Father's concerns instead of his own self-interest. For this perfect humility, the Father exalted him to the highest place and gave him the name which is above all names (see Philippians 2:9-11).

This same Jesus is with us today, encouraging us to be humble so that God can exalt us along with him. We need this encouragement because we tend to think quite highly of ourselves. Pride about who we are and what we have prevents God from bringing us into a deeper union with him. Almighty God has made us free so that we can choose to love him better than ourselves. When we admit our need for God, his work of lifting us up can begin.

As people who desire to follow Jesus as our Master, we need to be aware of the ways we operate out of pride. There is so much in our human nature that prevents us from acknowledging our true condition. Without even noticing it, we count ourselves great in the kingdom of God. Recognizing these attitudes can be a doorway to deeper union with Christ as we seek to follow him.

"Heavenly Father, we have no works worthy of you. Help us to be humble as we await your work in us."

Luke 14:12-14

12 He said also to the man who had invited him, "When you
give a dinner or a banquet, do not invite your friends or your
brothers or your kinsmen or rich neighbors, lest they also invite
you in return, and you be repaid. 13 But when you give a feast,
invite the poor, the maimed, the lame, the blind, 14 and you will
be blessed, because they cannot repay you. You will be repaid at
the resurrection of the just."

Jesus' instruction to his host was to care for the poor and needy—not just those who would "pay him back" for his kindness. It's easy to do nice things for those we care about or those who will repay us. But Jesus wants us to reach out to the poor, the lame, and the blind—to people who could never repay our kindness.

Jesus loved the poor and identified with them: "Though he was rich . . . he became poor" (2 Corinthians 8:9). Born in a stable and raised in a remote village, he lived simply. During his life, he lacked even a permanent place to lay his head. Then, he died in poverty on the cross. Jesus identified with the poor so deeply that he said we care for him every time we care for the needy (see Matthew 25:34-40).

We find Christ in the poor, the sick, and the lonely. A prayer offered daily by Mother Teresa's helpers in Calcutta expresses this: "Though you hide yourself behind the unattractive disguise of the irritable, the exacting, and the unreasonable, may I still recognize you and say, 'Jesus, my patient, how sweet it is to serve you.' " For those who love Jesus, it is a thrill to actually touch him by caring for the poor.

Jesus wants us to have hearts like his. We don't have to perform grand and heroic works; the simple things will suffice. We can visit a lonely neighbor, bring food to the homebound, join with a group visiting prisons, or serve at a hospice. Most churches and communities sponsor outreach missions that we can take part in. If we see a need that's not being addressed by others, we can organize services ourselves. Let us touch the heart of Jesus by serving those who cannot repay us. In this way, we begin to imitate Jesus.

"Jesus, set my heart aflame for your precious poor. May I encounter you each time I help these, your beloved sons and daughters."

Luke 14:15-24

15 When one of those who sat at table with him heard this, he
said to him, "Blessed is he who shall eat bread in the kingdom of
God!" 16 But he said to him, "A man once gave a great banquet,
and invited many; 17 and at the time for the banquet he sent his
servant to say to those who had been invited, 'Come; for all is
now ready.' 18 But they all alike began to make excuses. The first
said to him, 'I have bought a field, and I must go out and see it; I

pray you, have me excused.' 19 And another said, 'I have bought
five yoke of oxen, and I go to examine them; I pray you, have me
excused.' 20 And another said, 'I have married a wife, and
therefore I cannot come.' 21 So the servant came and reported
this to his master. Then the householder in anger said to his
servant, 'Go out quickly to the streets and lanes of the city, and
bring in the poor and maimed and blind and lame.' 22 And the
servant said, 'Sir, what you commanded has been done, and still
there is room.' 23 And the master said to the servant, 'Go out to
the highways and hedges, and compel people to come in, that my
house may be filled. 24 For I tell you, none of those men who
were invited shall taste my banquet.' "

Jesus' love is so great that he wants everyone to participate in the banquet of his victory over death. He offers to all the bread that does not perish, the bread of life given for the world (see John 6:48-51). It is a great honor to be invited to this banquet.

According to Middle Eastern etiquette of the time, guests to a banquet were invited in advance. Then, when the feast was ready, a second notification was sent telling them that all was prepared. To refuse to attend at the time of the second invitation was considered extremely impolite. It would have been an even greater insult for the guests to have used the excuses they did, pleading activities that could have been done at some other time.

The honored guests in the parable represented the Pharisees and the rulers of Israel, the leaders of God's people who initially accepted God's invitation by the obedience to the law, yet declined the second invitation by refusing to accept Jesus as Savior. The second group of people, those in the streets and lanes of the city (Luke 14:21), represented the general Jewish population, those who did not bear responsibility for the whole nation. The third group those in the highways and hedges (14:23), were the Gentiles, all the neighboring peoples who were aliens and unbelievers. Clearly, God excluded nobody from the invitation.

How often we feel that we aren't important enough or perhaps good enough for God to work in our lives. We think that he wants us to become better people, to do away with all our faults and sins before he will even approach us. But the truth is that the bread from heaven is available to everyone.

Jesus' love and mercy are so great that his invitation is without limitations: "Behold, I stand at the door and knock; if any one hears my voice and opens the door, I will come in to him and eat with him, and he with me" (Revelation 3:20). He so wants us to attend his banquet that he told his servants to "compel people to come in" that his house, his heavenly dwelling, may be filled (Luke 14:23).

"Lord Jesus, I want to be present at your banquet, despite my sin and unworthiness. By the power of your Holy Spirit, I accept your generous invitation to the heavenly banquet."

Luke 14:25-35

25 Now great multitudes accompanied him; and he turned and
said to them, 26 "If any one comes to me and does not hate his
own father and mother and wife and children and brothers and
sisters, yes, and even his own life, he cannot be my disciple.
27 Whoever does not bear his own cross and come after me,
cannot be my disciple. 28 For which of you, desiring to build a
tower, does not first sit down and count the cost, whether he has
enough to complete it? 29 Otherwise, when he has laid a
foundation, and is not able to finish, all who see it begin to

mock him, 30 saying, 'This man began to build, and was not able
to finish.' 31 Or what king, going to encounter another king in
war, will not sit down first and take counsel whether he is able
with ten thousand to meet him who comes against him with
twenty thousand? 32 And if not, while the other is yet a great
way off, he sends an embassy and asks terms of peace.
33 So therefore, whoever of you does not renounce all that he has
cannot be my disciple.
34 "Salt is good; but if salt has lost its taste, how shall its saltness
be restored? 35 It is fit neither for the land nor for the dunghill;
men throw it away. He who has ears to hear, let him hear."

Large crowds were now following Jesus as he moved on toward his fate in Jerusalem. In order to teach them the full meaning of discipleship, Jesus spoke quite boldly: "If any one comes to me and does not hate father and mother, wife and children, brothers and sisters, yes, and even life itself, he cannot be my disciple" (Luke 14:26). The thought of "hating" one's family and one's own life might appear to be at odds with Jesus' all-embracing command to love. But Jesus was using a form of exaggeration that was common in Semitic preaching. "Hate" in this sense means to prefer less, not to despise outright.

Because Jesus talked like this to stress a point, we take his point very seriously: True disciples must renounce anyone or anything that stands in the way of a thorough commitment to Jesus. Jesus used two examples to illustrate the mature deliberation and unswerving commitment that discipleship calls for. A wise builder would not begin a project without the necessary resources to complete it. Similarly, only a foolish king would send his soldiers into battle unless he was prepared, without hesitation, to commit himself fully to the demands of such an undertaking.

These examples illustrate how important it is that Jesus' followers establish their priorities properly. Saying that discipleship to Jesus is a priority, while remaining encumbered by other competing concerns or relationships, is practicing a false—and ultimately useless—discipleship.

As Jesus' disciples, we can ask the Holy Spirit to teach us how to order and prioritize our lives so that the demands of the gospel do not conflict with the concerns of our family and our own well-being. The Father has given us the kingdom—his own life and nature. The more we learn to order our lives according to his nature in us, the more stable and balanced our lives will become. Tensions between the call of the gospel and our practical responsibilities may arise, but God allows them in order to teach us to rely more deeply on his wisdom and leave our own ways behind.

"Holy Spirit, we look to you for guidance and wisdom. Continue to fill us with God's presence and power. Teach us to maintain the various aspects of our lives in good order as we wait expectantly for Jesus' return."

Mercy and Justice

LUKE
15–16

Luke 15:1-10

1 Now the tax collectors and sinners were all drawing near to
hear him. 2 And the Pharisees and the scribes murmured, saying,
"This man receives sinners and eats with them."
3 So he told them this parable: 4 "What man of you, having a
hundred sheep, if he has lost one of them, does not leave the
ninety-nine in the wilderness, and go after the one which is lost,
until he finds it? 5 And when he has found it, he lays it on his
shoulders, rejoicing. 6 And when he comes home, he calls
together his friends and his neighbors, saying to them, 'Rejoice
with me, for I have found my sheep which was lost.' 7 Just so, I tell
you, there will be more joy in heaven over one sinner who repents
than over ninety-nine righteous persons who need no repentance.
8 "Or what woman, having ten silver coins, if she loses one coin,
does not light a lamp and sweep the house and seek diligently until
she finds it? 9 And when she has found it, she calls together her
friends and neighbors, saying, 'Rejoice with me, for I have found
the coin which I had lost.' 10 Just so, I tell you, there is joy before
the angels of God over one sinner who repents."

We are the Lord's—we belong to him (see Romans 14:8). We are the crowning joy of his creation (see Genesis 1:31). Most of us cannot imagine ourselves giving delight to the Creator of the universe simply because we exist. We are more apt to allow guilt and preoccupation with our shortcomings and sins to overshadow the security God wants us to have in his unconditional love.

God is preoccupied with what is lost—missing from his kingdom—so that he can bring them back to him. He cares when, like the sheep in Jesus' parable, we stray from obedience to him, because he knows that we risk experiencing loss, pain, or distress. Jesus, the Good Shepherd, is deeply aware of our suffering, and he longs to bring us relief. How he loves to find the lost! How he longs to hold us tenderly in his arms!

To teach this lesson to the Pharisees—who prided themselves on their legalism and looked down on the tax collectors and "sinners"—Jesus told of a shepherd who had one hundred sheep. Only one strayed. The shepherd didn't curse it for wandering away, or abandon it to the wolves. Leaving all the others, he earnestly sought out the stray. Our practical minds might ask: "Why risk ninety-nine for the sake of one?" But Jesus wants to make it clear how precious each one of us is to God. We are all worth the risk that the shepherd took: Jesus sacrificed his own life for us by dying on the cross. It confounds the mind to think that he would have made the very same sacrifice had only one—any one—of us fallen into sin.

Each of us, in some way, at some time in our lives, becomes lost. We all stray (see Isaiah 53:6). We also can experience Jesus' gentleness and compassion every time we turn to him in repentance. He never tires of forgiving us! He never tires of seeking us out and returning us to his flock. He only asks that we remain humble and strive to follow him. He will never condemn us for wandering from him, or for getting lost, if our heart's desire is to love him. We may be weak, but he is strong.

"Father, thank you for your extravagant love for us. Thank you for the good and gentle Shepherd you have given to watch over us. May we learn humility and the joy of repentance. Protect us and encourage us in our love for you."

Luke 15:11-32

11 And he said, "There was a man who had two sons; 12 and
the younger of them said to his father, 'Father, give me the share
of property that falls to me.' And he divided his living between
them. 13 Not many days later, the younger son gathered all he
had and took his journey into a far country, and there he
squandered his property in loose living. 14 And when he had
spent everything, a great famine arose in that country, and he
began to be in want. 15 So he went and joined himself to one of
the citizens of that country, who sent him into his fields to feed
swine. 16 And he would gladly have fed on the pods that the
swine ate; and no one gave him anything. 17 But when he came
to himself he said, 'How many of my father's hired servants have
bread enough and to spare, but I perish here with hunger!
18 I will arise and go to my father, and I will say to him, "Father, I
have sinned against heaven and before you; 19 I am no longer
worthy to be called your son; treat me as one of your hired
servants.' " 20 And he arose and came to his father. But while he
was yet at a distance, his father saw him and had compassion,
and ran and embraced him and kissed him. 21 And the son said
to him, 'Father, I have sinned against heaven and before you; I
am no longer worthy to be called your son.' 22 But the father
said to his servants, 'Bring quickly the best robe, and put it on
him; and put a ring on his hand, and shoes on his feet; 23 and
bring the fatted calf and kill it, and let us eat and make merry;
24 for this my son was dead, and is alive again; he was lost, and is
found.' And they began to make merry.
25 "Now his elder son was in the field; and as he came and
drew near to the house, he heard music and dancing. 26 And he
called one of the servants and asked what this meant. 27 And he
said to him, 'Your brother has come, and your father has killed
the fatted calf, because he has received him safe and sound.'
28 But he was angry and refused to go in. His father came out

and entreated him, 29 but he answered his father, 'Lo, these
many years I have served you, and I never disobeyed your
command; yet you never gave me a kid, that I might make
merry with my friends. 30 But when this son of yours came, who
has devoured your living with harlots, you killed for him the
fatted calf!'
31 And he said to him, 'Son, you are always with me, and all
that is mine is yours. 32 It was fitting to make merry and be
glad, for this your brother was dead, and is alive; he was lost,
and is found.' "

The famous parable of the prodigal son gives us a glimpse of our heavenly Father's heart, full of love for each of us. We are his wayward children who have sinned and fallen short of his glory in so many ways. And he is our merciful Father, always ready to welcome us when we return to him in repentance.

How much the Father loves us! So much so that he gave each of us a free will to love him or reject him. It's our choice. Even when we choose to reject him and his ways, and experience the consequences of our sin, God still loves us and longingly awaits our return. When we come to our senses, repent and return to him, he is there waiting for us. He doesn't wait until we've changed completely; he isn't looking for perfection. He just wants us to call on him.

The Father not only forgives his wayward children but he lavishes them with his gifts. St. Ambrose (c. 339-397)—reflecting on the return of the wayward son—wrote about what we all receive:

> "So quickly does he gain forgiveness that, as he is coming, and is still a great way off, his father meets him, gives him a kiss, which is the sign of sacred peace; orders the robe to

> be brought forth, which is the marriage garment, which if any one have not, he is shut out from the marriage feast; places the ring on his hand, which is the pledge of faith and the seal of the Holy Spirit; orders the shoes to be brought out, for he who is about to celebrate the Lord's Passover, about to feast on the Lamb, ought to have his feet protected against all attacks of spiritual wild beasts and the bite of the serpent; bids the calf to be slain, for 'Christ our Passover has been sacrificed' " (*Concerning Repentance*, Book 2, 3.18).

God does not make us prove that we are worthy. The only thing that is important to him is that once we were dead in our sin, and now we are alive through the precious blood of Jesus. We are more important to our heavenly Father than anything we have done. His love and mercy are so great that there is no sin he won't forgive.

"Father, I come to you acknowledging that I have sinned against you. I am not worthy to be your child. Yet, trusting in your love and mercy, I ask your forgiveness. Father, I want to come home to your embrace."

Luke 16:1-8

1 He also said to the disciples, "There was a rich man who had
a steward, and charges were brought to him that this man was
wasting his goods. 2 And he called him and said to him, 'What
is this that I hear about you? Turn in the account of your
stewardship, for you can no longer be steward.' 3 And the
steward said to himself, 'What shall I do, since my master is
taking the stewardship away from me? I am not strong enough to

dig, and I am ashamed to beg. [4] I have decided what to do, so
that people may receive me into their houses when I am put out
of the stewardship.' [5] So, summoning his master's debtors one by
one, he said to the first, 'How much do you owe my master?'
[6] He said, 'A hundred measures of oil.' And he said to him, 'Take
your bill, and sit down quickly and write fifty.' [7] Then he said to
another, 'And how much do you owe?' He said, 'A hundred
measures of wheat.' He said to him, 'Take your bill, and write
eighty.' [8] The master commended the dishonest steward for his
prudence; for the sons of this world are wiser in their own
generation than the sons of light.

Sometimes, we might not be clear about the point Jesus was trying to make when he told a parable or gave a sermon. The parable of the shrewd manager can be one of these cases. We know that Jesus was not condoning dishonesty or irresponsibility. And he surely didn't want to promote shady business dealings. So what was his purpose in telling this story? How do we apply it to our lives?

When we find ourselves stumped by scripture, we can always ask the Holy Spirit to open our hearts and minds to understand his revelation. By praying in this way, we can affirm our belief that God the Father wants to give us all good things if we ask him. We can also refer to a biblical commentary or study-Bible for further background. These tools can teach us about the cultural context of Jesus' time so that we can better understand the images and examples he used in teaching the people.

During Jesus' time, the type of steward described in the passage often earned his wages from the interest he charged his master's customers. Often, stewards would charge exorbitant interest as a way of creating a comfortable "buffer zone" for themselves against future misfortune. By reducing his master's debtors' bills, the steward was not cheating his master; he was reducing his own profit. Thus, with the debtors grateful to him for reducing their bills, the steward had new friends who could help him start a new life. From this perspective, the steward's action could be seen as an attempt to reform his life—and a very creative approach to a difficult problem. Rather than commending the steward's seeming dishonesty, Jesus was actually highlighting his ability to think quickly and overcome major obstacles.

How tempting it can be to give up when we encounter obstacles to daily prayer, evangelization, or reaching out to our neighbors! But with the example of the shrewd manager, we can take comfort that Jesus wants to help us find creative solutions to these obstacles. We can become just as shrewd as this steward, asking God to give us uncommon wisdom and the courage to take risks in new situations.

"Father, by the power of your Spirit, please give us the wisdom and creativity to overcome any obstacles that prevent us from responding to your will."

Luke 16:9-15

9 And I tell you, make friends for yourselves by means of
unrighteous mammon, so that when it fails they may receive you
into the eternal habitations.
10 "He who is faithful in a very little is faithful also in much;
and he who is dishonest in a very little is dishonest also in much.
11 If then you have not been faithful in the unrighteous
mammon, who will entrust to you the true riches? 12 And if you
have not been faithful in that which is another's, who will give
you that which is your own? 13 No servant can serve two

masters; for either he will hate the one and love the other, or he will be devoted to the one and despise the other. You cannot serve God and mammon."
14 The Pharisees, who were lovers of money, heard all this, and they scoffed at him. 15 But he said to them, "You are those who justify yourselves before men, but God knows your hearts; for what is exalted among men is an abomination in the sight of God."

In the parable of the shrewd manager (Luke 16:1-8), Jesus spoke about ingenuity and creativity in stewardship. As he went on to explain this parable, he made a connection between being trustworthy "in very little"—things here on earth—and being trustworthy when it comes to the greater treasures of heaven. Jesus knows that the ones who are shrewd and generous in the use of their money and time will naturally have the same qualities when they set themselves to serving the Lord and his people. Here, as in so many other instances, we see how powerfully God's grace can build on human nature.

Because he knows us intimately, God meets each of us according to our situations. He never asks us to do more than we are able—and he does not often ask us to do less than we are able. We need not fear that we will be unable to bear the responsibilities he gives us, either in worldly matters or in spiritual matters. He is a loving Father, not a stern taskmaster waiting to punish us. God has given us a helper, the Holy Spirit, to teach us how to be reliable stewards. He only asks that we seek godly wisdom to manage our affairs properly. Over time, he will entrust us with heavenly treasures.

Simon Peter is an excellent example of God's patience. Jesus promised him the keys to the kingdom long before Peter was ready to receive them. He could do this because he saw Peter not as he was, but as he would be. He knew that one day Peter would be able to bear the responsibility, and he told Peter so that he could prepare himself.

Even when this "rock" of the church denied his Master three times (Matthew 16:18; 26:69-75), Jesus did not take the keys away from him. Rather, he forgave Peter and continued to teach him and strengthen him. Over time, we see Peter boldly preaching the gospel, wisely guiding the church, and ultimately laying down his life for the One who had trusted him so completely. As Peter became more trustworthy, he also became more of a servant—a true steward of grace.

"Heavenly Father, thank you for your promise of true riches in heaven. Give us the grace that we need each day to live wholly surrendered to you so that we can be your most trusted friends both here on earth and in heaven."

Luke 16:16-18

16 "The law and the prophets were until John; since then the
good news of the kingdom of God is preached, and every one
enters it violently. 17 But it is easier for heaven and earth to pass
away, than for one dot of the law to become void.
18 "Every one who divorces his wife and marries another
commits adultery, and he who marries a woman divorced from
her husband commits adultery."

Jesus set a new standard of righteousness when he preached the good news of the kingdom of God (Luke 16:16). The law and the prophets were not wiped away by the coming of the kingdom—instead they were perfected and fulfilled. They now reflect the Father's deepest desires for humanity. Through the grace bestowed on us by Christ's death and resurrection, we can take up our true inheritance as sons and daughters of God. Through repentance and forgiveness, hearts can be changed, cleansed, and made new.

An example of the newness of life in the kingdom is manifested in Jesus' words on marriage and divorce. In those days, a man could obtain a divorce from his wife relatively easily. The Mosaic law stated that a man could write his wife a bill of divorce if "she finds no favor in his eyes because he has found some indecency in her" (Deuteronomy 24:1). One school of rabbinic thought interpreted this to mean that the only justification for divorce was adultery. However, another school, which was widely gaining favor, said that a man could obtain a divorce for nearly any reason. On the other hand, a woman could almost never divorce her husband. The laxness of this second interpretation threatened family life.

Jesus' words shed light on God's desire for men and women, whom he wanted to be committed and faithful partners in marriage. Men and women were meant to share a permanent and irrevocable communion of life and love. God created man and woman to become one flesh (see Genesis 2:24). Marriage is meant to reflect the union that God himself desires with his people—a union so intimate that it must not be broken.

The Mosaic law was a concession to the Israelites because of their hard hearts (see Mark 10:5). But Jesus' death and resurrection have made us a new people—restored and united with Christ so that we can live in a way that is consistent with God's plan for his people. When we embrace the power of Jesus, then the impossible becomes a reality. In spite of the sin and temptation that can destroy family life, we have not been left alone. Jesus wants to help us and strengthen us in our resolve. We can experience healing and peace in our relationships with one another.

"Lord, we entrust all marriages to your love and protection. Raise up these unions in you to become wonderful signs of God's love for his people everywhere."

Luke 16:19-31

[19] "There was a rich man, who was clothed in purple and fine
linen and who feasted sumptuously every day. [20] And at his gate
lay a poor man named Lazarus, full of sores, [21] who desired to be
fed with what fell from the rich man's table; moreover the dogs
came and licked his sores. [22] The poor man died and was carried
by the angels to Abraham's bosom. The rich man also died and
was buried; [23] and in Hades, being in torment, he lifted up his
eyes, and saw Abraham far off and Lazarus in his bosom. [24] And
he called out, 'Father Abraham, have mercy upon me, and send
Lazarus to dip the end of his finger in water and cool my tongue;
for I am in anguish in this flame.' [25] But Abraham said, 'Son,
remember that you in your lifetime received your good things,
and Lazarus in like manner evil things; but now he is comforted
here, and you are in anguish. [26] And besides all this, between us
and you a great chasm has been fixed, in order that those who
would pass from here to you may not be able, and none may
cross from there to us.' [27] And he said, 'Then I beg you, father,
to send him to my father's house, [28] for I have five brothers, so
that he may warn them, lest they also come into this place of
torment.' [29] But Abraham said, 'They have Moses and the
prophets; let them hear them.'
[30] And he said, 'No, father Abraham; but if some one goes to

them from the dead, they will repent.' [31] He said to him, 'If they do not hear Moses and the prophets, neither will they be convinced if some one should rise from the dead.' "

God our Father wants each one of us to be with him for eternity in an embrace of mutual love. Since love can only be given freely, God gives us the freedom to cling to him or turn away from him. And, day after day, he provides us with opportunities to use our freedom.

This was the case with the rich man and the beggar in Jesus' parable. Their circumstances were entirely different, but God loved them equally and offered both of them opportunities to love him. Lazarus, as St. John Chrysostom observed, had the choice of bearing his condition with patience and trust in God. The rich man had the choice of relieving Lazarus' pain.

As it turned out, Lazarus cooperated with God's purposes; the rich man did not. He had "Moses and the prophets," that is, scripture. And, more importantly, he had Lazarus at his gate. Day after day, Lazarus' presence was a God-given invitation for the rich man to lay aside his selfish desires and respond to a fellow human being in need. Because the rich man refused God's love, he ended up in misery. He became the beggar, while Lazarus entered eternity with the Lord.

As a young nun, St. Thérèse de Lisieux was asked to care for an elderly sister. This older nun complained about everything Thérèse did for her. But Thérèse trusted that the Father was using this situation to forge a love in her heart that she could not generate by her own power. God was offering her his heart! Every day, the Lord provides us with similar situations where we can lay aside our selfish desires and embrace Jesus through caring for our brothers and sisters. The Father wants to give us new hearts that delight in his ways.

"Father, thank you for your perfect love for me. I give you my heart so that you can work through me as you want. I long to be with you forever!"

The Outcast and the Dedicated

Luke
17:1–19:27

Luke 17:1-6

1 And he said to his disciples, "Temptations to sin are sure to
come; but woe to him by whom they come! 2 It would be better
for him if a millstone were hung round his neck and he were cast
into the sea, than that he should cause one of these little ones to
sin. 3 Take heed to yourselves; if your brother sins, rebuke him,
and if he repents, forgive him; 4 and if he sins against you seven
times in the day, and turns to you seven times, and says, 'I
repent,' you must forgive him."
5 The apostles said to the Lord, "Increase our faith!" 6 And
the Lord said, "If you had faith as a grain of mustard seed, you
could say to this sycamine tree, 'Be rooted up, and be planted in
the sea,' and it would obey you."

As Jesus continued his journey toward Jerusalem (Luke 9:51-19:44), he taught his disciples what it meant to follow him. It was inevitable, he told them, that there would be stumbling blocks to faith, both because of Satan's interference, and because of the all-too-human tendency to abuse our freedom. But the inevitability of such temptations and abuses doesn't excuse our need to be vigilant against sin and to continue to uphold one another in dignity and love.

To be a disciple of Jesus means to pay close attention to the forces that move in our hearts, to determine whether they are coming from the Spirit or from the drives of our fallen nature. We must also be on guard against temptations from other people, all the while holding out love and mercy for everyone. We are called to love even those who hurt us and provoke improper reactions from us.

Using the graphic image of the millstone, Jesus told his disciples that it would be better to die than to be the source of another person's sin. Then, approaching the same teaching from another angle, he taught them to forgive and lovingly correct those who lead others into sin. This is especially important when those who are hurt are the "little ones" (Luke 17:2)—the weak and vulnerable for whom Jesus has a special concern.

Reeling under the impact of these demands, the disciples asked Jesus to increase their faith. Jesus assured them that faith would prove adequate to the demands because of God's great desire to establish his kingdom among his people. This has been his purpose from the beginning of time, and he is committed to bringing it about. Even the smallest amount of faith can achieve what is humanly impossible. "If you had faith as a grain of mustard seed, you could say to this sycamine tree, 'Be rooted up, and be planted in the sea,' and it would obey you" (Luke 17:6). No obstacle, no matter the size, can stand before faith in God. No obstacle can prevent the humble from living in mercy and love, just as Jesus did.

"Lord Jesus, we believe that you came to establish your kingdom among us. Through the gift of faith you have bestowed on us, we happily embrace the opportunities you give us to love your people. Lord, increase our faith so that we may build your kingdom."

Luke 17:7-10

7 "Will any one of you, who has a servant plowing or keeping
sheep, say to him when he has come in from the field, 'Come
at once and sit down at table? 8 Will he not rather say to him,
'Prepare supper for me, and gird yourself and serve me, till I eat
and drink; and afterward you shall eat and drink? 9 Does he
thank the servant because he did what was commanded?

[10] So you also, when you have done all that is commanded you, say, 'We are unworthy servants; we have only done what was our duty.' "

At first glance, Jesus' words to his disciples might seem quite harsh. Essentially, he told them that if they just do what he commands, they are "unworthy servants." So, was he expecting them to slave even harder? Was he telling them that if they just did a little bit more, they'd be "worthy" servants who merited his pleasure? No. God is never indebted to us. We owe God everything, even our very lives. We were created for him, not he for us.

Jesus' parable shines a light on the kind of discipleship that he is calling us to, not the amount of work he's looking for. We can choose to be servants responding to him like slaves, or we can follow him in love and gratitude like friends. Jesus wants to call us his friends (see John 15:15), not his slaves. He wants us to know him as our brother, as the most loyal companion we will ever have.

Have you ever thought about how easily we could work for God and yet never really know him? We could do all sorts of work for the church and the poor, either out of a sense of duty or out of a desire to ensure our place in heaven. But if we respond to God this way, we've missed the point. He is calling us to a relationship of love, not one of slavery. Those who think like duty-bound slaves miss out on a wonderful experience of life in the kingdom of God. They won't know a relationship with Jesus that can fill them so deeply that they long to give everything back to him.

Of course, there are things we must do as his disciples. Jesus has told us to obey his commandments. But, there are things that we do for Jesus just because we love him—like turning our hearts to him during a busy day or going out of our way to help one of his little ones. Let us respond to Jesus out of love today. Let us ask the

Holy Spirit to fill our hearts with God's love so that his love for us would awaken our love for him.

"Jesus, thank you for giving your life for us. We praise you because of what you did on the cross. Now, we freely give our lives back to you."

Luke 17:11-19

11 On the way to Jerusalem he was passing along between
Samaria and Galilee. 12 And as he entered a village, he was met
by ten lepers, who stood at a distance 13 and lifted up their voices
and said, "Jesus, Master, have mercy on us." 14 When he saw
them he said to them, "Go and show yourselves to the priests."
And as they went they were cleansed. 15 Then one of them,
when he saw that he was healed, turned back, praising God with
a loud voice; 16 and he fell on his face at Jesus' feet, giving him
thanks. Now he was a Samaritan. 17 Then said Jesus, "Were not
ten cleansed? Where are the nine? 18 Was no one found to
return and give praise to God except this foreigner?"
19 And he said to him, "Rise and go your way; your faith has
made you well."

In Jesus' time, those suffering from leprosy were isolated in special camps outside the cities in an effort to contain the disease. According to Jewish law, the only way a leper could be allowed to return to society was if he or she were declared clean by the priests (see Leviticus 14).

Jesus' command that these ten lepers show themselves to the priests required that they act in faith since, at the outset of the journey, they had not yet been healed. There was also at least one foreigner—one who wasn't a Jew—among the group. Therefore, to demand an action in keeping with the Jewish law would in itself be a challenge and could have offended the foreigners. The one Samaritan who returned had to overcome considerable obstacles in order to follow Jesus' request. How his obedience to Jesus, and his worship and gratitude for his healing, must have pleased the Lord!

The Greek word used in this passage to describe how the Samaritan approached Jesus—"giving him thanks"—is *eucharisteo*, the same root for the word Eucharist, and it has the sense of thanksgiving for an unmerited gift. The more we ponder everything that the Eucharist is meant to do in us—cleanse our hearts before God, free us from the power of sin, and unite us as one body in Christ—the more we would find joy and thanksgiving welling up in our hearts.

This is the attitude that the Lord loves to see whenever his children gather to celebrate the Eucharist. And, it is an attitude that can bring us even deeper healing. Jesus told the Samaritan: "Rise and go your way, your faith has made you well" (Luke 17:19). Were not the other nine healed? Certainly. But this grateful Samaritan received a healing that far surpassed the physical cleaning of his skin. The wholeness he received in his flesh pointed to the wholeness he was receiving in his heart as he knelt before the Lord in worship. Like this Samaritan, let us lay our hearts bare before the Lord and allow him to bring us deeper healing and wholeness.

"Lord Jesus, we believe that your desire to work in us far surpasses our expectations. We come to you today asking you to transform us. Jesus, we bow before you in praise and thanksgiving."

Luke 17:20-25

20 Being asked by the Pharisees when the kingdom of God was
coming, he answered them, "The kingdom of God is not coming
with signs to be observed; 21 nor will they say, 'Lo, here it is!' or
'There!' for behold, the kingdom of God is in the midst of you."
22 And he said to the disciples, "The days are coming when you
will desire to see one of the days of the Son of man, and you will
not see it. 23 And they will say to you, 'Lo, there!' or 'Lo, here!'
Do not go, do not follow them. 24 For as the lightning flashes
and lights up the sky from one side to the other, so will the Son
of man be in his day. 25 But first he must suffer many things and
be rejected by this generation."

The Pharisees who asked when the kingdom of God would come showed that they still didn't understand what this kingdom meant. They couldn't see that it was already in their midst. The blind were seeing, the deaf were hearing, the lame were walking—Who could miss these signs? Yet because they could not accept what Jesus was about, the Pharisees did miss them. And we might too, if we are not open to the movement of the Holy Spirit in our lives.

The kingdom of God is dynamic, powerful, and noticeable. From the very beginning of the church, people's lives have been radically impacted by the gospel. In every age—including our own—God has moved in mighty ways, revealing his love, rescuing his people from sin, and transforming even the hardest of hearts. Whenever God moves, wherever his presence is welcomed by his people, powerful things occur: Miracles take place, and people are healed. And these external miracles are only the beginning, for they testify to God's presence among his people. From the external, God moves to the internal, changing lives and healing relationships.

When God acts, it is often like lightning flashing from one end of the sky to another; you can't miss it. At times when we do not sense his presence, we can still trust that he is with us. In his divine wisdom, God may "hide himself" from us in order to draw us closer to him. Perhaps we have become self-sufficient or have begun to look to other sources for what only God can give us. Ever merciful, God calls us back.

We only have to ask God to show himself to us, to ask Jesus to reveal his love and the power of his gospel. If our hearts are true and faithful, God will move in us. We can have great hope and assurance that we can know God in a deep and personal way. Jesus suffered and died for us, and his death and resurrection have removed the barriers that keep us from God. He is our Father, and he wants to bless us.

"Lord Jesus, we look for your movement in the world today. We ask you to begin in your church and in our hearts. Move so powerfully that our lives would be radically transformed by the gospel and so that we would become shining witnesses to your kingdom."

Luke 17:26-37

[26] As it was in the days of Noah, so will it be in the days of the
Son of man. [27] They ate, they drank, they married, they were
given in marriage, until the day when Noah entered the ark, and
the flood came and destroyed them all. [28] Likewise as it was in
the days of Lot—they ate, they drank, they bought, they sold,
they planted, they built, [29] but on the day when Lot went out
from Sodom fire and brimstone rained from heaven and
destroyed them all— [30] so will it be on the day when the Son of
man is revealed. [31] On that day, let him who is on the housetop,

with his goods in the house, not come down to take them away;
and likewise let him who is in the field not turn back. [32]
Remember Lot's wife. [33] Whoever seeks to gain his life will lose
it, but whoever loses his life will preserve it. [34] I tell you, in that
night there will be two men in one bed; one will be taken and
the other left. [35] There will be two women grinding together;
one will be taken and the other left." [37] And they said to him,
"Where, Lord?" He said to them, "Where the body is, there the
eagles will be gathered together."

Throughout Jesus' journey to Jerusalem, he sought to teach his disciples what it means to follow him and to allow his life to penetrate their hearts. Part of his teaching centered not only on his approaching death, but also upon the promise that he would come again at the end of time to establish his kingdom. In a sense, everything Jesus said and did was meant to prepare us for the end of time. His greatest desire is to gather us all together in him and establish us in his Father's presence forever.

Teaching the disciples how to live in preparation for that day, he reminded them of how unprepared people were in the days of Noah and Lot. They were captured by their needs and the things of the world. They had ignored God and wandered away from the obedience of faith. It is interesting to note that Jesus did not even mention the wicked deeds of those days. It was enough simply to say that they were not ready because they did not recognize the saving grace of God. This, after all, is the root of all sin and evil. When our hearts remain open to God's presence, we are protected from temptation and sin. It is when we wander away from him that we find ourselves lured into the darkness. To be prepared for the Lord's return means that we seek to remain open to God—through prayer, his word, and humble obedience.

Jesus taught his disciples that when the day comes for him to return in glory, it will come quickly and powerfully. In every age, he calls his disciples to be prepared to go with the Lord to the heavens without looking back. This is true whether it happens on the day the Lord returns, or at the time of our death.

How can we prepare ourselves? Through living faith in Jesus, the Son of Man. As we turn to Jesus in our hearts, he gives us the grace to live for him and to be willing to let go of this earthly life. His Spirit in us gives us the power to "lose" our lives and so preserve them in him. While we may live in this world and use its goods, they should not have a claim on our hearts. We belong to Jesus, and we can trust that he will come for us and bring us into eternal life with him.

"Thank you, Lord, for the gift of faith through which we know you and are saved. Help us to let go of anything that binds us to the world so that we can live for you more and more each day."

Luke 18:1-8

1 And he told them a parable, to the effect that they ought
always to pray and not lose heart. 2 He said, "In a certain city
there was a judge who neither feared God nor regarded man;
3 and there was a widow in that city who kept coming to him and
saying, 'Vindicate me against my adversary.' 4 For a while he
refused; but afterward he said to himself, 'Though I neither fear
God nor regard man, 5 yet because this widow bothers me, I will
vindicate her, or she will wear me out by her continual coming.' "
6 And the Lord said, "Hear what the unrighteous judge says.
7 And will not God vindicate his elect, who cry to him day and
night? Will he delay long over them? 8 I tell you, he will

vindicate them speedily. Nevertheless, when the Son of man comes, will he find faith on earth?"

What is your view of God? Do you think of him as an unjust judge? Do you think you must cajole him into caring for you? How easy it is for us to misunderstand the way God works! How quickly we develop false perceptions based on the way we interpret the events in our lives. Yet, the truth still stands that our God is loving and just. We can count on him to give us all that we need.

The judge in this parable was unscrupulous. According to Jewish law (see Deuteronomy 24:17-22), the widow had every right to ask for help. In fact, the judge should have given her request priority. Instead, however, he refused her again and again and made her beg for justice. In contrast, God is just, faithful, and loving. While we may not see immediate answers to our prayers, we should not despair. There are times when he delays so that he can teach us about trust. There are also times when the answer we think is best might actually hurt us.

It can be difficult to abandon our cares to God. We cannot expect to understand why and how God chooses to answer our prayers—we do not know his divine purposes. But we can look to Jesus to show us the way to trust and obedience. Jesus fully turned his life over to God. Even in the midst of tremendous physical, emotional, and spiritual suffering, he embraced God's will. As a result, he was raised up and exalted to the highest place in heaven.

We can all know the love of God that Jesus knew. Let us pray persistently and wait to see how God will respond to us in love. God loves us. When something doesn't work out the way we had planned, let us not despair or begin blaming God. Let us reflect on Jesus' example and abandon our lives to God. The Father had the best in mind for Jesus and he has the best in mind for us—even through the most difficult circumstances. We can trust God. His love always prevails.

"Father, forgive us when we entertain thoughts that you are unjust or unloving toward us. We are weak and cannot understand your ways. Help us in our weakness—strengthen us as we persist in our prayer."

Luke 18:9-14

9 He also told this parable to some who trusted in themselves
that they were righteous and despised others: 10 "Two men went
up into the temple to pray, one a Pharisee and the other a tax
collector. 11 The Pharisee stood and prayed thus with himself,
'God, I thank thee that I am not like other men, extortioners,
unjust, adulterers, or even like this tax collector. 12 I fast twice a
week, I give tithes of all that I get.' 13 But the tax collector,
standing far off, would not even lift up his eyes to heaven, but
beat his breast, saying, 'God, be merciful to me a sinner!' 14 I tell
you, this man went down to his house justified rather than the
other; for every one who exalts himself will be humbled, but he
who humbles himself will be exalted."

How important it is to understand that we are saved by grace through faith! This was the fundamental difference between the Pharisee and the tax collector in Jesus' parable. The Pharisee believed that he would be justified by his own works, while the tax collector realized that he was a sinner and that his only hope was in God's mercy. What a difference these attitudes can make in the way we live!

If we put ourselves in the Pharisee's place, we would constantly be reminding God how hard we have worked to please him; we would expect him to reward us for our labors. Notice that the Pharisee didn't even ask for mercy! On the other hand, if we stood in the shoes of the tax collector, we would realize that we don't have—and cannot earn—righteousness on our own. We are justified only by God's grace through the merits of Jesus. Our foundation would be sure because Jesus paid the price for our sin, and we would not feel as if we had to make deals with God.

If we could have earned righteousness on our own merit, Jesus would not have had to die on the cross. But, because we were separated from God by sin and unable to save ourselves, God sent his only Son to pay our penalty. Only through his perfect suffering could we be forgiven and be brought back into God's presence.

How should such truths impact our conduct? Knowing that Jesus has already won our salvation can relieve us of many burdens. We are already accepted by the Father if we but turn to him and rely on his grace to free us from sin. This is far different than striving to win heaven by our own merits, where every failure brings fear of condemnation, and every success brings pride and self-righteousness. Praise God that whenever we exercise our faith in our salvation, we grow in confidence and joy. We desire to love and obey God more, and we are more eager to share this good news with everyone we meet. Let us imitate the tax collector and continue to make God's mercy and love the foundation for our lives.

"Lord Jesus, by your death and resurrection you have redeemed us for God. Your all-encompassing love for us surpasses all measure. Help us to live by faith today and every day."

Luke 18:15-17

15 Now they were bringing even infants to him that he might
touch them; and when the disciples saw it, they rebuked them.
16 But Jesus called them to him, saying, "Let the children come
to me, and do not hinder them; for to such belongs the kingdom
of God. 17 Truly, I say to you, whoever does not receive the
kingdom of God like a child shall not enter it."

Madam, you have wonderful children, and we're honored that you'd like Jesus to be the one to bless them. . . ." So probably began at least one of Jesus' disciples as he attempted to shoo away a group of children brought before them by their parents. He continued: "Please understand, Jesus is a very busy man, proclaiming a deeply spiritual message that even adults find difficult to grasp. Can't the town rabbi perform the blessing you seek? I'm sure that would be something he is happy and prepared to do."

In spite of the concerns voiced by his disciples, Jesus made a special effort to speak with and bless children. Before this incident, no religious leader or philosopher in history had ever considered children to be so important. After the children were gone, Jesus used the incident to teach the disciples some foundational elements about the kingdom of God.

First, Jesus clearly legitimized the parents' desire to have their children blessed. Somehow Jesus attached value even to a blessing which to most would seem to have less than top priority in spiritual importance. Secondly, and perhaps more importantly, Jesus showed that he welcomes any movement to be close to him. Children are not looking to bless others, but to be blessed. Children come empty-handed, desiring only to be near to Jesus.

And that simple response is one that Jesus cherishes most.

Luke reported that Jesus made those remarks as they were heading toward Jerusalem. As Christ taught his disciples about his coming death and resurrection, he used this and other passages to make it clear that the kingdom of God is a gift we inherit, not something we earn. We can see the tenderness Jesus has for children. As we accept our role as children of God, we should never doubt that the Father has the same love and tenderness for us as Jesus demonstrated for the youngsters who flocked to him.

"Lord Jesus, thank you for taking the time to show the world how deeply our Father loves us. May his tenderness soften my heart and change me within. And may that new heart change those I come into contact with, including my own children."

Luke 18:18-23

18 And a ruler asked him, "Good Teacher, what shall I do to
inherit eternal life?" 19 And Jesus said to him, "Why do you call
me good? No one is good but God alone. 20 You know the
commandments: 'Do not commit adultery, Do not kill, Do not
steal, Do not bear false witness, Honor your father and mother.' "
21 And he said, "All these I have observed from my youth."
22 And when Jesus heard it, he said to him, "One thing you still
lack. Sell all that you have and distribute to the poor, and you
will have treasure in heaven; and come, follow me." 23 But when
he heard this he became sad, for he was very rich.

At times, we can be like this wealthy ruler, thinking of God as a judge who only loves us if we are good enough. Our human nature causes us to think that by being "perfect" or doing good things, we can somehow earn his approval. In Jesus' response to the ruler, however, we can see that what our Lord really wants are hearts set on loving him.

We can sometimes miss the point of Jesus' ministry as we busily attend to all our responsibilities for the church, our families, and those in need. God assuredly wants us to do good works in his name. But the obedience which truly pleases God comes from hearts full of love for him. Even if we did try to earn our way into heaven, we could not. The ruler stumbled because he thought that he could gain eternal life by fulfilling the law. He couldn't see that God is concerned primarily about our interior disposition.

We too will misstep if we focus on dogged external obedience rather than on loving God. By loving Jesus, we come to understand that we are saved by God's grace (see Ephesians 2:8). The revelation of his love—and the love that this revelation calls forth from our hearts—will move us to do away with those things that displease him. It will move us to become like him in his generosity and compassion. We may not have to sell our possessions. All we have to do is soften our hearts to God a little more each day. As we do, God supplies the grace we need to obey his commands.

Ask yourself: "Do I think that what I do will get me into heaven, or do I trust in the power of Jesus' cross to save me? Am I more concerned with obedience to God's laws, or with allowing his love to change my heart?" If your answers to these questions are not as you would like, don't despair: We all fall short of loving the Lord as we should. But God patiently helps us as we seek him in love.

"Father, help me to surrender my heart to Jesus. I believe that his death and resurrection are the way to eternal life. I want you to become the passion and treasure of my heart."

Luke 18:24-30

[24] Jesus looking at him said, "How hard it is for those who
have riches to enter the kingdom of God! [25] For it is easier for a
camel to go through the eye of a needle than for a rich man to
enter the kingdom of God." [26] Those who heard it said, "Then
who can be saved?" [27] But he said, "What is impossible with
men is possible with God." [28] And Peter said, "Lo, we have left
our homes and followed you." [29] And he said to them, "Truly, I
say to you, there is no man who has left house or wife or brothers
or parents or children, for the sake of the kingdom of God,
[30] who will not receive manifold more in this time, and in the
age to come eternal life."

In ancient times, it was generally understood that God blessed those he loved with prosperity—and to those who sinned, he brought ruin. The disciples must have been amazed when Jesus told them of the pitfalls of riches. Didn't wealth signify friendship with God? For those who trust in their own abilities or wealth, it can be very difficult to turn to the Lord. Jesus was explaining that our Father wants hearts that burn with love for him alone. Such hearts would have to keep possessions and wealth in the right perspective.

Those who cast themselves on Jesus are willing to part with anything that gets in the way of their relationship with the Lord. Possessions, position in life, and even relationships must be less important to us than God. These things cannot save us. In some cases, they can help us draw closer to God, but they can hinder us just as easily. It all depends on whether our hearts are set on the Lord.

The seekers of wealth that Jesus spoke of are the independent and self-reliant of this world. They place great importance upon their possessions and power, and perhaps in the esteem of other people as well. But in the Sermon on the Mount, Jesus said: "Blessed are the poor in spirit, for theirs is the kingdom of heaven" (Matthew 5:3). The Father wants his children to look to him for everything. He wants children who will acknowledge their sins and ask for forgiveness through his Son. He wants children who will acknowledge their weaknesses and ignorance, and who will rely upon him alone for guidance and strength.

Jesus knew that it was impossible for us to renounce the things of this world and look to God alone for our needs. This is what he meant when he said, "What is impossible with men is possible with God" (Luke 18:27). Let us ask God to do the impossible. Only he can make our hearts burn with love for him. Let us go to him and ask for his help in turning away from any worldly concern that competes with him for our love and attention.

"Jesus, come purify our hearts from earthly attachments. Send your Holy Spirit to burn in our hearts so that we can love the Father above everything else."

Luke 18:31-43

31 And taking the twelve, he said to them, "Behold, we are going
up to Jerusalem, and everything that is written of the Son of man
by the prophets will be accomplished. 32 For he will be delivered
to the Gentiles, and will be mocked and shamefully treated and
spit upon; 33 they will scourge him and kill him, and on the third
day he will rise." 34 But they understood none of these things; this
saying was hid from them, and they did not grasp what was said.
35 As he drew near to Jericho, a blind man was sitting by the
roadside begging; 36 and hearing a multitude going by, he
inquired what this meant. 37 They told him, "Jesus of Nazareth is
passing by." 38 And he cried, "Jesus, Son of David, have mercy
on me!" 39 And those who were in front rebuked him, telling

him to be silent; but he cried out all the more, "Son of David,
have mercy on me!" 40 And Jesus stopped, and commanded him
to be brought to him; and when he came near, he asked him,
41 "What do you want me to do for you?" He said, "Lord, let me
receive my sight." 42 And Jesus said to him, "Receive your sight;
your faith has made you well." 43 And immediately he received
his sight and followed him, glorifying God; and all the people,
when they saw it, gave praise to God.

In narrating Jesus' final journey to Jerusalem (Luke 9:51-19:44), Luke drew together a number of Jesus' teachings on what it meant to be true disciples. In these chapters, Jesus taught his followers how to pray to the Father with the confidence of little children (18:16-17), and to know their worth in God's eyes (12:32). Above all, he desired that they would come to obey God out of love, rather than scrupulously following rules, as many of the Pharisees did (10:26-28).

Time and again, the disciples witnessed Jesus' unfailing tenderness and his incomparable power, even though their understanding of who he was remained quite dim. Now, as they approached Jericho on the last stage of their journey, a blind beggar who had heard about Jesus cried out for help. Jesus called him forward and healed him on the spot. In response to this miracle of restoration, the man "followed him, glorifying God" (Luke 18:43). On the surface, it seems like just another miracle story. However, if we ask the Spirit to show us, we can discern wonderful depths here that can teach us much about discipleship.

Luke used this story to illustrate that not only was the man's physical sight restored, but the eyes of his heart were opened as well. It's as if Luke were telling his readers: "Open your eyes and see Jesus. He has so much he wants to show you about why he gave his life for you. This is why he went to Jerusalem: To become the sacrificial Lamb of God whose blood would free you from sin and darkness. As they traveled to Jerusalem, even the disciples failed to grasp this vital fact (Luke 18:34).

The blind man did not follow Jesus because it was the right thing to do. Rather, his heart was captivated by the One who had healed him, and he happily joined him. As we open our hearts to the Lord to receive his love and healing, we too will be captivated. This is a true disciple—not one who follows because it's expected, but one whose heart has been captured by Jesus and who will abandon everything for the sake of inheriting his kingdom.

"Jesus, we come to you as the blind man did, without hesitancy or fear. Open the eyes of our hearts so we might see you in all your purity, love, and faithfulness. Jesus, Son of David, have mercy on us!"

Luke 19:1-10

1 He entered Jericho and was passing through. 2 And there was
a man named Zacchaeus; he was a chief tax collector, and rich.
3 And he sought to see who Jesus was, but could not, on account
of the crowd, because he was small of stature. 4 So he ran on
ahead and climbed up into a sycamore tree to see him, for he was
to pass that way. 5 And when Jesus came to the place, he looked
up and said to him, "Zacchaeus, make haste and come down; for I
must stay at your house today." 6 So he made haste and came
down, and received him joyfully. 7 And when they saw it they all
murmured, "He has gone in to be the guest of a man who is a
sinner." 8 And Zacchaeus stood and said to the Lord, "Behold,
Lord, the half of my goods I give to the poor; and if I have
defrauded any one of anything, I restore it fourfold." 9 And Jesus

said to him, "Today salvation has come to this house, since he also is a son of Abraham. [10] For the Son of man came to seek and to save the lost."

As a tax-collecting puppet of the Roman government, and as one who regularly defrauded honest, sincere children of Abraham, Zacchaeus was branded by his fellow Jews as a sinner for whom there was no hope. Imagine how surprised Jesus' followers would have been to see Jesus not only talk with Zacchaeus, but invite himself to this tax collector's home for dinner. No wonder many of the Pharisees were scandalized. There seemed to be no limit to the kinds of people Jesus would consort with!

This is one of the most important points Luke made throughout his gospel. Jesus looks beyond the external appearance, into the heart of every man and woman. There, he sees each person's need for the love of God. Deep in his heart, Zacchaeus must have cried out: "There must be more to life than this!" He was rich in material goods, but he was lonely and empty of the love that only God could give. How thrilled he must have been to be able to welcome Jesus into his home. He responded by giving half of his belongings to the poor and promising to pay back fourfold anyone whom he had defrauded. Such extravagance went far beyond the requirements of Jewish law. It simply flowed out of a grateful heart.

Jesus knows our hearts. He knows our sorrows—for he weeps with us. He knows our joys—for he rejoices with us. God knows everything about us, even our weaknesses. In fact, he uses these weaknesses to draw us to him. He knows that when we are needy we are more open to accepting God's love. It is in our weakness that we realize that no matter what we have done, God still loves us, still wants to speak to us. He is always standing at the door of our hearts, asking us to let him in.

When we answer Jesus' invitation and welcome him into our hearts, we are filled with joy, because only Jesus can fill that deepest part of our being. It is often the very situation that has caused us pain that most opens us up to Jesus: Like Zacchaeus, our desire for him becomes a desperation to be freed from anything that cuts us off from his presence.

"Lord Jesus, we invite you into our hearts. Come and fill us with the joy of your salvation. Grant us the freedom to lay at your feet every possession or desire that we have considered more precious than you."

Luke 19:11-27

[11] As they heard these things, he proceeded to tell a parable,
because he was near to Jerusalem, and because they supposed
that the kingdom of God was to appear immediately. [12] He said
therefore, "A nobleman went into a far country to receive
kingly power and then return. [13] Calling ten of his servants, he
gave them ten pounds, and said to them, 'Trade with these till I
come.' [14] But his citizens hated him and sent an embassy after
him, saying, 'We do not want this man to reign over us.'
[15] When he returned, having received the kingly power, he
commanded these servants, to whom he had given the money, to
be called to him, that he might know what they had gained by
trading. [16] The first came before him, saying, 'Lord, your pound
has made ten pounds more.' [17] And he said to him, 'Well done,
good servant! Because you have been faithful in a very little, you
shall have authority over ten cities.' [18] And the second came,
saying, 'Lord, your pound has made five pounds.' [19] And he said
to him, 'And you are to be over five cities.' [20] Then another
came, saying, 'Lord, here is your pound, which I kept laid away

in a napkin; 21 for I was afraid of you, because you are a severe
man; you take up what you did not lay down, and reap what you
did not sow.' 22 He said to him, 'I will condemn you out of your
own mouth, you wicked servant! You knew that I was a severe
man, taking up what I did not lay down and reaping what I did
not sow? 23 Why then did you not put my money into the bank,
and at my coming I should have collected it with interest?'
24 And he said to those who stood by, 'Take the pound from him,
and give it to him who has the ten pounds.' 25 (And they said to
him, 'Lord, he has ten pounds!') 26 'I tell you, that to every one
who has will more be given; but from him who has not, even
what he has will be taken away. 27 But as for these enemies of
mine, who did not want me to reign over them, bring them here
and slay them before me.'"

In the parable of the investments (Luke 19:11-27), Jesus told his disciples that the time would come when he will ask for an accounting. The disciples' expectations about Jesus entering Jerusalem as a mighty king, and their hopes of sharing in his reign, had to be replaced by the call to service and humble stewardship. Like the nobleman in the parable, Jesus will receive his kingdom, but he will also entrust his servants with much and expect a good return on all that he invested in them.

Each of us has been given much. In addition to material blessings, we all have received gifts that cannot be seen with the natural eye. Through the sacrament of Baptism, God washed away the stain of original sin and gave us the dignity of citizenship in his kingdom. Whenever we receive the Eucharist with open hearts, Jesus is free to work powerfully in us, conforming us to his image. We even have the Holy Spirit—the indwelling life and love of God—who daily seeks to increase our share of divine life and to bring us to a deeper faith and experience of the mysteries of Christ.

What have we done with the gifts he has given us? Have we nurtured them through prayer, scripture reading, and the sacraments? Have we tried to bring others to the same knowledge of God's love by sharing the gospel with them? Have we allowed his Spirit to purify us ever more fully of all sin? Life in the kingdom of God is both a high privilege and a demanding calling: to love and worship God and to love and serve our brothers and sisters.

Because we are working in our Father's kingdom, we do not work with purely human wisdom or human effort. We will not be judged by whether we have worked hard enough. Rather, we will be asked whether we have allowed the Spirit to work through us. He is the giver of gifts, the revealer of truth, and the power of God active in human hearts.

"Father, help us to surrender our human wisdom so that your wisdom may unfold within us. We willingly embrace the way in which you have called us to serve. Holy Spirit, multiply your gifts in us and empower us, that your glory would be made manifest to everyone we meet."

A Devotional Commentary on Luke

Jesus in Jerusalem

Luke
19:28–21:38

Luke 19:28-40

28 And when he had said this, he went on ahead, going up to
Jerusalem. 29 When he drew near to Bethphage and Bethany, at
the mount that is called Olivet, he sent two of the disciples,
30 saying, "Go into the village opposite, where on entering you
will find a colt tied, on which no one has ever yet sat; untie it
and bring it here. 31 If any one asks you, 'Why are you untying
it?' you shall say this, 'The Lord has need of it.' " 32 So those who
were sent went away and found it as he had told them. 33 And as
they were untying the colt, its owners said to them, "Why are you
untying the colt?" 34 And they said, "The Lord has need of it."
35 And they brought it to Jesus, and throwing their garments on
the colt they set Jesus upon it. 36 And as he rode along, they
spread their garments on the road. 37 As he was now drawing
near, at the descent of the Mount of Olives, the whole multitude
of the disciples began to rejoice and praise God with a loud voice
for all the mighty works that they had seen, 38 saying, "Blessed is
the King who comes in the name of the Lord! Peace in heaven
and glory in the highest!" 39 And some of the Pharisees in the
multitude said to him, "Teacher, rebuke your disciples." 40 He
answered, "I tell you, if these were silent, the very stones would
cry out."

From a Sermon by St. Andrew of Crete:

Let us go together to meet Christ on the Mount of Olives. Today he returns from Bethany and proceeds of his own free will toward his holy and blessed passion, to consummate the mystery of our salvation. He who came down from heaven to raise us from the depths of sin, to raise us with himself, we are told in

Scripture, *above every sovereignty, authority and power, and every other name that can be named*, now comes of his own free will to make his journey to Jerusalem. He comes without pomp or ostentation. As the psalmist says: *He will not dispute or raise his voice to make it heard in the streets*. He will be meek and humble, and he will make his entry in simplicity.

Let us run to accompany him as he hastens toward his passion, and imitate those who met him then, not by covering his path with garments, olive branches or palms, but by doing all we can to prostrate ourselves before him by being humble and by trying to live as he would wish. Then we shall be able to receive the Word at his coming, and God, who no limits can contain, will be within us.

In his humility Christ entered the dark regions of our fallen world and he is glad that he became so humble for our sake, glad that he came and lived among us and shared in our nature in order to raise us up again to himself. And even though we are told that he has now ascended above the highest heavens—the proof, surely, of his power and godhead—his love for man will never rest until he has raised our earthbound nature from glory to glory, and made it one with his own in heaven.

So let us spread before his feet, not garments of soulless olive branches, which delight the eye for a few hours and then wither, but ourselves, clothed in his grace, or rather, clothed completely in him. We who have been baptized into Christ must ourselves be the garments that we spread before him. Now that the crimson stains of our sins have been washed away in the saving waters of baptism and we have become white as pure wool, let us present the conqueror of death, not with mere branches of palms but with the real rewards of his victory. Let our souls take the place of the welcoming branches as we join today in the children's holy song: *Blessed is he who comes in the name of the Lord. Blessed is the King of Israel.*

Luke 19:41-44

41 And when he drew near and saw the city he wept over it,
42 saying, "Would that even today you knew the things that make
for peace! But now they are hid from your eyes. 43 For the days
shall come upon you, when your enemies will cast up a bank
about you and surround you, and hem you in on every side,
44 and dash you to the ground, you and your children within you,
and they will not leave one stone upon another in you; because
you did not know the time of your visitation."

When he drew near and saw the city he wept over it. (Luke 19:41)

As Jesus stood overlooking the city of Jerusalem, he knew that not everybody would accept the salvation he had come to bring to the world. This was true of many in Jerusalem, and Jesus knew that the city would pay a price for its rejection of him. Jesus' lament for Jerusalem is reminiscent of the words of Jeremiah when he prophesied the destruction of the city before the exile some six centuries earlier (see Jeremiah 6). Many also see Jesus' words as a prophecy of Jerusalem's destruction at the hands of the Roman army in 70 A.D.

Jesus' concern for the city is emphasized by *klaio*, the Greek word for "weep" used in Luke 19:41 which expresses a depth of anguish and sorrow beyond the normal. The same word is used to describe the anguish Peter experienced when he realized that he had denied Jesus (see Matthew 26:75), the remorse of the woman who anointed Jesus' feet in her repentance for her sins (Luke 7:38), and the sorrow of the people over the death of a young girl (see Mark 5:38). Jesus cried bitter tears as he thought of the fate of the city because of the hardheartedness of the people.

Jerusalem saw Jesus as an enemy as he confronted the city's legalism and lack of belief. Nonetheless, Jesus offered peace and reconciliation to the people of God, and their rejection caused him great sorrow. He is the only path to peace; those who do not acknowledge him come to war and destruction, both within themselves and against their world (see Matthew 11:20-24).

Jesus did not come to condemn the world but to save it (see John 3:16-17). He loves us so much that he willingly became a suffering servant, a man "despised and rejected" (see Isaiah 53:3), to bring about our redemption. Instead of condemning us, he suffered pain and humiliation on the cross so that we could realize the promise of eternal life. Some—despite this good news—chose to live for themselves and reject salvation, and it was for these that Jesus mourned.

"Lord Jesus, I want to be among those who accept you and the salvation you bring. I am grateful for your love and want to respond to your invitation to life. Save me from destruction and bring me into the glory of your presence."

Luke 19:45-48

45 And he entered the temple and began to drive out those
who sold, 46 saying to them, "It is written, 'My house shall be a
house of prayer'; but you have made it a den of robbers."
47 And he was teaching daily in the temple. The chief priests
and the scribes and the principal men of the people sought to
destroy him; 48 but they did not find anything they could do, for
all the people hung upon his words.

We normally think of Jesus as very pious and mild-mannered. Somehow, the picture of him turning over tables, throwing money to the floor, and chasing people out of the temple is harder for us to imagine. But Jesus could never tolerate abuse of his Father's purposes. The leaders of his people had become unjust and dishonest, turning the temple into a place to do business and make profits. Yahweh was no longer honored, and this moved Jesus to take aggressive action to purify his Father's house.

Luke tells us that once he had driven out the moneychangers, Jesus spent every day in the temple teaching (Luke 19:47). If the temple was to become a place of prayer again, it would be with Jesus at its center, teaching the people about what it meant to live in his Father's presence.

Just as he did in the temple, Jesus wants to do in our lives. He wants to teach the gift and privilege of prayer, making our hearts houses of prayer where his Father is honored. With this goal in mind, Jesus wants to drive sin out of our hearts and remove everything that stands as an obstacle to him. He wants to take up residence within our hearts to such an extent that we are always praying, even as we go about the many demands of our lives.

Jesus wants to do more than teach us to pray: He wants to make his home in our hearts and minds. All we have to do is welcome him and ask him to teach us. We can take comfort in the knowledge that this is something Jesus deeply desires to do in us. He wants to fill each of us with his presence. In fact, he wanted this so much that he gave up his own life in order to take away the sin that separated us from him. Now, through the power of the Holy Spirit, he wants to cleanse us of sin and fill us with his love. Nothing could be more encouraging.

"Jesus, thank you for dying for our sins. Come into our lives. Take your rightful place at the center of our hearts. Cleanse us of all sin and make us pure dwelling places. Be with us every day to comfort, fill us with peace and joy, and empower us to do your will."

Luke 20:1-8

1 One day, as he was teaching the people in the temple and
preaching the gospel, the chief priests and the scribes with the
elders came up 2 and said to him, "Tell us by what authority
you do these things, or who it is that gave you this authority."
3 He answered them, "I also will ask you a question; now tell
me, 4 Was the baptism of John from heaven or from men?"
5 And they discussed it with one another, saying, "If we say,
'From heaven,' he will say, 'Why did you not believe him?'
6 But if we say, 'From men,' all the people will stone us; for
they are convinced that John was a prophet." 7 So they
answered that they did not know whence it was. 8 And Jesus
said to them, "Neither will I tell you by what authority I do
these things."

Jesus lived a life filled with God's peace and joy; yet, as we know, it was not an easy life. In addition to the suffering he chose to bear for our sins, he continually withstood opposition from religious leaders who were determined to trick him into saying or doing something incriminating.

Jesus knew the blindness of the hardhearted who opposed him. Each time they tried to trick him or accuse him, however, he always responded with wisdom, not only silencing his accusers, but offering them opportunities to repent and accept his message. Consider some of his responses: "Let him who is without sin among you be the first to throw a stone" (John 8:7). "Why do you ask me about what is good? One there is who is good. If you would enter life, keep the commandments" (Matthew 19:17). "Render to Caesar the things that are Caesar's, and to God the things that are God's" (Mark 12:17).

Jesus often refused to answer questions directly, responding instead in ways that unmasked unbelief and silenced the "wise" men of his day. He responded to his opponents, not in anger or bitterness, but with the wisdom and love that came from his intimate relationship with his heavenly Father (see John 5:20). His life of prayer and his attentiveness to the leading of the Holy Spirit were the source of his love, wisdom, and strength.

None of us is immune to rejection, accusation, or persecution as we seek to follow Jesus. Through his death and resurrection, however, we are a new creation and have been brought close to the Father's heart. By seeking deeper intimacy with the Lord through prayer, the liturgy, and scripture, we can learn to respond to others—even our accusers—with God's love and wisdom. As we turn to the Lord, asking for wisdom and hearts of love, we open ourselves to the transforming power of the Spirit and can become more like Jesus himself, who always spoke the truth in love.

"Lord Jesus, we acknowledge that apart from you we can do nothing. Transform our hearts and draw us closer to our heavenly Father. O Spirit of God, guide us, lead us, and empower us to live each day in ways pleasing to you."

Luke 20:9-18

9 And he began to tell the people this parable: "A man
planted a vineyard, and let it out to tenants, and went into
another country for a long while. 10 When the time came, he
sent a servant to the tenants, that they should give him some of
the fruit of the vineyard; but the tenants beat him, and sent him
away empty-handed. 11 And he sent another servant; him also
they beat and treated shamefully, and sent him away empty-
handed. 12 And he sent yet a third; this one they wounded and

cast out. 13 Then the owner of the vineyard said, 'What shall I
do? I will send my beloved son; it may be they will respect him.'
14 But when the tenants saw him, they said to themselves, 'This
is the heir; let us kill him, that the inheritance may be ours.' 15
And they cast him out of the vineyard and killed him. What
then will the owner of the vineyard do to them? 16 He will come
and destroy those tenants, and give the vineyard to others."
When they heard this, they said, "God forbid!" 17 But he looked
at them and said, "What then is this that is written: 'The very
stone which the builders rejected has become the head of the
corner'? 18 Every one who falls on that stone will be broken to
pieces; but when it falls on any one it will crush him."

Jesus used the parable of the tenants to foretell the fate of the Jews who would reject him. The landowner in this parable represents God, and the vineyard symbolizes his people Israel (see Isaiah 5:1-7). The tenant farmers represent the various religious and political leaders of Israel, and the harvest time is when God will call the Israelites to account for their actions.

The servants are the prophets who were mistreated or killed because they spoke the truth regarding Israel's rebellion against God. The son, of course, represents Jesus, who knew that shortly he too would be rejected by the Jews. The Jewish leaders were rejecting Jesus, whom God had sent to become the "cornerstone" of their lives. Jesus quoted scripture to show that this would happen (see Luke 21:17; Psalm 118:23).

The Pharisees and the chief priests knew that Jesus was speaking about them. In their time, they were considered exemplary "builders" of a holy life, but they were trying to build it out of their own virtue and strength rather than through true conversion of heart to God. Without this true conversion, they rejected God and his Son Jesus Christ, the cornerstone and way to the Father.

We must consider how Jesus is speaking to us through this parable. We too must know that we either accept Jesus as the cornerstone for our lives or we will find him to be a rock over which we will stumble (see 1 Peter 2:6-8). Jesus will be the cornerstone in our lives if we recognize him as the one sent by the Father to teach us and lead us in the ways of truth. Do we see Jesus as central in our lives and try to follow him each day by being obedient to what he teaches in scripture and through the church? Do we turn to him in both daily personal prayer and when we gather as a body for the liturgy? These are signs which can indicate whether Jesus is the cornerstone in our lives.

"Lord Jesus, I want you to be the cornerstone of my life so that whatever undertakings I make will never shake or crumble. Holy Spirit, help me to understand what it means to have Jesus as my cornerstone and to know that all that is lasting is built on him."

Luke 20:19-26

19 The scribes and the chief priests tried to lay hands on him at
that very hour, but they feared the people; for they perceived
that he had told this parable against them. 20 So they watched
him, and sent spies, who pretended to be sincere, that they
might take hold of what he said, so as to deliver him up to the
authority and jurisdiction of the governor. 21 They asked him,
"Teacher, we know that you speak and teach rightly, and show
no partiality, but truly teach the way of God. 22 Is it lawful for us
to give tribute to Caesar, or not?" 23 But he perceived their
craftiness, and said to them, 24 "Show me a coin. Whose likeness

and inscription has it?" They said, "Caesar's." [25] He said to them, "Then render to Caesar the things that are Caesar's, and to God the things that are God's." [26] And they were not able in the presence of the people to catch him by what he said; but marveling at his answer they were silent.

Render to Caesar the things that are Caesar's,
and to God the things that are God's. (Luke 20:25)

When the spies of the scribes and chief priests questioned Jesus about whether it was "lawful to give tribute to Caesar," Jesus knew they were setting a trap for him. The tax issue was real for the Jewish people: Was it right to pay taxes to the occupying Roman forces? Yet Jesus could see beyond the question to the intentions of those who posed it. If he answered "yes," he could be accused of collaborating with the enemy. If he answered "no," the Herodians could accuse him of rebellion.

Jesus avoided this trap ingeniously by asking them to produce a Roman coin. He pointed to the image of Caesar on the coin and told them to give to Caesar what is Caesar's and to God what is God's (Luke 20:25).

Most of us pay taxes, giving to our government what is the government's due. In a similar way, we are called to give to God the things that are his—our hearts, our minds and wills, and our lives. Because we are God's beloved children, Jesus' statement is not so much a challenge as it is an invitation to give our whole selves to him. Our lives themselves are a gift from the Lord, and in love we can offer this gift back to our Creator.

In truth, even our material possessions and our money are given to us by God. But as we give our hearts to him, he leads us—through the Holy Spirit, the wisdom of scripture, and the teachings of the church—to live righteously in every detail of our lives. God's wisdom for our lives can be very practical, including even the political, social and financial decisions we may face.

Like the Roman coin, we too have been "stamped" with an image—the image of God (see Genesis 1:27). God loved us so much that he created us to be like him, to be filled with his "strength and beauty" (Psalm 96:6). Because we are the image of God, we have the privilege of hearing him call us each by name (see Isaiah 45:4).

"Lord, by your Spirit, allow us to see your strength and beauty in others. Remove anything that might hinder us from giving ourselves to you in purity and in love. Help us, Lord, to reflect your love more fully each day."

Luke 20:27-40

27 There came to him some Sadducees, those who say that
there is no resurrection, 28 and they asked him a question,
saying, "Teacher, Moses wrote for us that if a man's brother dies,
having a wife but no children, the man must take the wife and
raise up children for his brother. 29 Now there were seven
brothers; the first took a wife, and died without children; 30 and
the second 31 and the third took her, and likewise all seven left
no children and died. 32 Afterward the woman also died. 33 In
the resurrection, therefore, whose wife will the woman be? For
the seven had her as wife."
34 And Jesus said to them, "The sons of this age marry and are
given in marriage; 35 but those who are accounted worthy to
attain to that age and to the resurrection from the dead neither
marry nor are given in marriage, 36 for they cannot die any more,
because they are equal to angels and are sons of God, being sons

of the resurrection. [37] But that the dead are raised, even Moses
showed, in the passage about the bush, where he calls the Lord
the God of Abraham and the God of Isaac and the God of Jacob.
[38] Now he is not God of the dead, but of the living; for all live to
him." [39] And some of the scribes answered, "Teacher, you have
spoken well." [40] For they no longer dared to ask him any
question.

The Sadducees were a group of religious leaders who, like the Pharisees, opposed Jesus. Unlike the Pharisees, however, they did not believe in a resurrection after death and held to the written Mosaic law as their sole source of authority. A stricter group than the Pharisees, they were deeply offended by Jesus' seemingly radical interpretation of scripture and the acceptance he extended to all people.

When Jesus began teaching in the temple courts, the Sadducees sent a group of representatives to try to trap him, thus discrediting him and his teaching. The hypothetical problem of the childless yet oft-married woman provided them with the bait for their trap. Was there a resurrection from the dead? How, then could Moses' teaching allow for such a puzzling situation?

Perceiving what lay behind their question, Jesus answered them on their own terms, but at the same time, he sought to raise their minds to heavenly truths. Consequently, he first presented a summary statement of his teachings, as rabbis traditionally did. To support his teaching, Jesus quoted the Torah itself (see Exodus 3:6; Luke 20:37), the only authority the Sadducees would accept.

But Jesus wanted to do more than just prove himself. While the form of his response corresponded to their tradition, its content was a radical departure. Not only are the righteous raised to life, they become "sons of God, being sons of the resurrection"

(Luke 20:36). The Father not only gives life on earth, but he sustains and even transforms life beyond the grave. Because death is conquered, the sons and daughters of the resurrection "cannot die any more;" they "live to him" (Luke 20:36,38) in a completely new life which transcends the life they knew on earth.

Jesus' answer, then, went beyond the Sadducees' questions to reveal the love and grace of the Father. As sons and daughters of the resurrection, we can experience the same life Jesus has, free from death and alive to God (see Romans 6:5-11). United with Jesus in faith and baptized into his death, we can know freedom from sin and death, the first fruits of the heavenly life that awaits us.

"Father, you are the author and sustainer of all life. By your Son's death and resurrection, you have promised us a transformed life in your presence. Through your Spirit, help us to be faithful as we anticipate the joys of eternal life."

Luke 20:41-47

41 But he said to them, "How can they say that the Christ is
David's son? 42 For David himself says in the Book of Psalms,
'The Lord said to my Lord, Sit at my right hand, 43 till I make
thy enemies a stool for thy feet.' 44 David thus calls him Lord; so
how is he his son?"
45 And in the hearing of all the people he said to his disciples,
46 "Beware of the scribes, who like to go about in long robes, and
love salutations in the market places and the best seats in the
synagogues and the places of honor at feasts, 47 who devour
widows' houses and for a pretense make long prayers. They will
receive the greater condemnation."

After fielding many questions from the Pharisees and Sadducees aimed at tricking him, Jesus asked them a question with the potential to transform their lives: How can the Christ be both son of David and David's Lord? Messianic prophesies foretold that the Christ would come from David's descendants (see 2 Samuel 7:12-16). This belief embodied the hope that the Messiah, anointed by Yahweh and coming from the line of the great King David, would bring lasting deliverance to Israel. Thus, Jesus quoted Psalm 110, where David identifies the Messiah as his Lord.

Why did Jesus present this riddle to the religious leaders? Was he just being philosophical? No. Jesus wanted to show that the messianic title, "son of David," failed to express his mystery fully. He was not just the Messiah sent by God to deliver his people. He is the Lord—God himself come to earth! In order for his hearers to accept this monumental truth in its fullness, they had to confront the labels they had placed on Jesus and the expectations that were underlying them.

We too must confront who we think Jesus is. Have we discovered him? Do we understand that he is the eternal God, Lord of creation, yet humbly united to our humanity? Pope John Paul II taught, "The Church wishes to serve this single end: that each person may . . . find Christ, in order that Christ may walk with each person the path of life" (*Redeemer of Man*, 13). Do we experience him walking with us in our days? He desires nothing more than to show himself to us. All he asks is that we seek him in prayer.

In its sacramental life, too, the church "lives his mystery, draws unwearyingly from it and continually seeks ways of bringing this mystery of her Master and Lord . . . every individual human being" (*Redeemer of Man*, 7). It is the Lordship of Jesus, revealed in its fullness through his death and resurrection, that has the power to transform each of our lives. It is this mystery that Jesus wanted to communicate to his hearers 2,000 years ago, and to us today.

"Holy Spirit, Lord and giver of life, reveal Jesus in my heart. Help me to surrender to the truth of his divine Lordship. May the fruits of his redemption be manifested in my life more fully."

Luke 21:1-4

1 He looked up and saw the rich putting their gifts into the
treasury; 2 and he saw a poor widow put in two copper coins.
3 And he said, "Truly I tell you, this poor widow has put in more
than all of them; 4 for they all contributed out of their
abundance, but she out of her poverty put in all the living that
she had."

How much is enough to give to God? A little when we can manage it? The same amount as what others give? Ten percent? Maybe more? The story of the widow's offering shows us two different answers to this question.

On the one hand, we see the rich contributing to the temple treasury out of their abundance. They had taken care of the necessities such as food, clothing, and shelter, and in addition had probably acquired a certain amount of "luxuries." Having made themselves comfortable, they were then willing to contribute to God. On the other hand, we see a poor widow, who had not provided for the necessities of life, let alone anything else, giving out of her poverty. She entrusted herself to God, believing that by seeking first his kingdom and his righteousness, she would have everything she needed (see Matthew 6:33). What excellent faith she had to trust God when she had nothing!

Luke's Gospel often portrays this theme of the exaltation of the poor and the humbling of the powerful. Through their poverty, the poor learn to depend on God and discover his generosity and his wealth. While the widow's extravagant giving may seem foolish to many, in God's eyes this sacrifice was more pleasing than those giving considerable amounts but with little sacrifice. The fact that Jesus recognized this widow's offering is an encouragement that Jesus recognizes our "small" sacrifices as well. He will never fail to care for his people.

The story of the widow's offering encourages us to humble ourselves before God. He loves us deeply and he wants to provide for us. He only asks that we surrender ourselves into his care. When she gave her small offering, the widow knew that God loved her and would take care of her. Therefore, she knew he was worthy of everything she had. The rich saw a God who was more distant and who therefore was not as worthy of the generosity that a beloved friend might deserve. Let us give our hearts to the Lord and allow him to care for our every need.

"Holy Spirit, help us to know the Lord in the same personal way as the poor widow did, so that we may offer him the same extravagant love. You are truly worthy of all we can give!"

Luke 21:5-11

5 And as some spoke of the temple, how it was adorned with
noble stones and offerings, he said, 6 "As for these things which
you see, the days will come when there shall not be left here one
stone upon another that will not be thrown down." 7 And they
asked him, "Teacher, when will this be, and what will be the sign
when this is about to take place?" 8 And he said, "Take heed that
you are not led astray; for many will come in my name, saying, 'I

am he!' and, 'The time is at hand!' Do not go after them. 9 And
when you hear of wars and tumults, do not be terrified; for this
must first take place, but the end will not be at once."
10 Then he said to them, "Nation will rise against nation, and
kingdom against kingdom; 11 there will be great earthquakes,
and in various places famines and pestilences; and there will be
terrors and great signs from heaven."

How often do we think about the end times? Do we believe and desire that Jesus will come again and that this will bring the Father's plan to completion? It is easy for us to lose sight of the big picture—of God's ultimate plan. We can be caught up in our day-to-day lives, in our jobs, our families, our troubles, and forget that one day Jesus will return in glory. Let us wait with eager expectation for Jesus' return by being faithful to him each day.

This prediction of the end times has at least two levels of meaning. On one level, Jesus was prophesying the destruction of Jerusalem and the temple by the Romans in 70 A.D. This is similar to Jeremiah's prophecy that the temple of Solomon would be destroyed because of the people's unfaithfulness to God (see Jeremiah 7). This happened in 586 B.C. when the Babylonians sacked Jerusalem.

On another level, Jesus was talking about the end of the world: "When you hear of wars and insurrections, do not be terrified; for these things must take place first, but the end will not follow immediately" (Luke 21:9). Jesus did not answer the disciples' question about when the end will come, but just said that wars and disasters will come first. We ourselves do not know the time or hour, nor can we prevent the events that must happen beforehand because they are part of God's plan.

What we can do, however, is to remain faithful to Jesus. If we stand firm in faith then these words of Jesus are hopeful. This is because we know that Jesus' return and the events that must precede it are part of God's eternal plan. Those who cling to Jesus and believe in him will experience eternal life when he comes, a life of fullness and joy beyond anything we can know in this earth-bound existence. For the unfaithful, however, these words are the occasion for sorrow.

Let us pray that we will always remain faithful to Jesus as we await his glorious return. "Heavenly Father, we trust in your plan that Jesus will come again in glory. Help us to remain faithful no matter what happens to us and around us. Pour out your grace upon the world so that all people will be ready to welcome Jesus when he returns. Come, Lord Jesus."

Luke 21:12-19

12 "But before all this they will lay their hands on you and
persecute you, delivering you up to the synagogues and prisons,
and you will be brought before kings and governors for my
name's sake. 13 This will be a time for you to bear testimony.
14 Settle it therefore in your minds, not to meditate beforehand
how to answer; 15 for I will give you a mouth and wisdom, which
none of your adversaries will be able to withstand or contradict.
16 You will be delivered up even by parents and brothers and
kinsmen and friends, and some of you they will put to death;
17 you will be hated by all for my name's sake. 18 But not a hair
of your head will perish. 19 By your endurance you will gain your
lives."

When Jesus said there would be persecution, he was revealing future events. By the time Luke was writing (some thirty years after Jesus had spoken), the abuse, harassment, and persecution which Jesus prophesied were widespread. Luke was describing the real life fulfillment of the Lord's words among the first generation of Christians.

Through the ages, Christians have been burned, beheaded, crushed, and fed to the wild beasts. This is what most of us picture when we hear the word "persecution." Historical and geographical distance have made suffering for our faith a remote concept for Christians living in Western societies. Persecution for us often takes various and sometimes subtle forms. It may be something as simple as being excluded from a social group, or being made fun of by friends and family. It might consist of being heckled at work when we try to stand up for our beliefs and principles.

Jesus speaks to every generation; Christians will always be persecuted, even by family members, because believing in Jesus and seeking to follow his teaching contradicts the ways of the world. Despite persecution, the Lord calls us to stand firm. He promises to protect and bless us in return for our faithfulness to him. Our faith will see us through, and it comes from the Lord alone. The writer of Hebrews called Jesus the "pioneer and perfecter of our faith" (Hebrews 12:2). He is the one who gives us faith and who strengthens our faith.

We must allow Jesus to come into the center of our lives. Is Jesus just an abstract idea to us? Do we only know him intellectually? Does he remain remote from our daily experience? If so, we will not be able to withstand persecution. Only a deep experience of Jesus and a personal knowledge of his love for us can enable us to stand with him in the face of persecution. This experience comes through the power of the Holy Spirit. We ought not worry about how to handle persecution. Jesus himself said: Do not worry about how to defend yourselves or what to say, because when the times comes, the Holy Spirit will teach you what to say (see Luke 12:11-12).

"Holy Spirit, raise me to the heavens where I may experience the revelation of my Savior. Reveal his love to me and make me single-hearted for him so that I will be able to proclaim him in the face of all persecution, however cruel or subtle."

Luke 21:20-28

[20] "But when you see Jerusalem surrounded by armies, then
know that its desolation has come near. [21] Then let those who
are in Judea flee to the mountains, and let those who are inside
the city depart, and let not those who are out in the country
enter it; [22] for these are days of vengeance, to fulfill all that is
written. [23] Alas for those who are with child and for those who
give suck in those days! For great distress shall be upon the earth
and wrath upon this people; [24] they will fall by the edge of the
sword, and be led captive among all nations; and Jerusalem will
be trodden down by the Gentiles, until the times of the Gentiles
are fulfilled.
[25] "And there will be signs in sun and moon and stars, and
upon the earth distress of nations in perplexity at the roaring of
the sea and the waves, [26] men fainting with fear and with
foreboding of what is coming on the world; for the powers of the
heavens will be shaken. [27] And then they will see the Son of
man coming in a cloud with power and great glory. [28] Now when
these things begin to take place, look up and raise your heads,
because your redemption is drawing near."

As he presented Jesus' teaching on the end times, Luke expanded the scope from Jerusalem and the temple (Luke 21:20-24) to encompass the whole of creation (21:25-27). And yet, even in the midst of such upheaval, Jesus encouraged them: "When these things begin to take place, look up and raise your heads, because your redemption is drawing near" (21:28). All these events are signs that Jesus' return is imminent, and for anyone who believes in him, such signs should bring joy and anticipation.

We can view the upheaval that we see in the world today as another sign pointing toward the final reality. We don't know when the end will come, but we do know that it will come in an unmistakable, recognizable way. Jesus told us: "There will be signs in sun and moon and stars, and upon the earth distress of nations in perplexity at the roaring of the sea and the waves" (Luke 21:25). Then, the end will come with Jesus' return as Judge.

How can we be sure that we will survive these times? Jesus promised: "God so loved the world that he gave his only Son, that whoever believes in him should not perish, but have eternal life" (John 3:16). While the coming judgment will cause many to faint "with fear and foreboding" (Luke 21:26), it can be a time of hope and encouragement for us. God wants to take away our fear of his judgment by planting the cross of Christ deep in our hearts. He wants to make us increasingly confident in the power of Jesus' salvation to keep us safe. The more we trust in God, relying on his Spirit's power to obey his commands, the less we will fear the coming judgment.

On the cross, Jesus paid the penalty for all our sins. In his resurrection, he poured out his Spirit to empower us to live in faith, obedience, and love. Let us accept Jesus more deeply into our lives. Let us ask him to give us the confidence to "look up" when the end comes and our redemption draws near.

"Jesus, we accept your great love for us. Keep us alert so that we will live each day for you and be ready for your coming."

Luke 21:29-33

29 And he told them a parable: "Look at the fig tree, and all
the trees; 30 as soon as they come out in leaf, you see for
yourselves and know that the summer is already near. 31 So also,
when you see these things taking place, you know that the
kingdom of God is near. 32 Truly, I say to you, this generation
will not pass away till all has taken place. 33 Heaven and earth
will pass away, but my words will not pass away."

Everyone has seen them; they're on street corners, at the beach, even at sporting events. You know, those wild-looking types waving signs proclaiming: *The end is here!* Most people give them a wide berth and casually ignore their message of doom. In some ways, to be closer to Jesus' teachings about the end times, they might paint new billboards announcing: *The beginning is here!*

Sitting in the temple, teaching the crowds, Jesus said: "Look at the fig tree, and all the trees; as soon as they come out in leaf, you see for yourselves and know that summer is already near. So also, when you see these things taking place, you know that the kingdom of God is near. Truly, I say to you, this generation will not pass away till all has taken place" (Luke 21:29-32). Jesus wanted his listeners to understand that they were witnessing the beginning of the messianic reign. The "end times" had begun.

It is a challenge to our faith to accept the seeming paradox that for the past two thousand years we have been living in the initial stages of Jesus' reign, that the fullness has yet to come. Yet this new era began when Jesus rose from the dead. In his resurrection, Jesus opened heaven for us. The entire created order has been altered to include a new relationship between God and his people in which heaven is brought to earth. We live in the age of the church, and as God's redeemed people, we can declare our victory over sin and death, even as we "wait in joyful hope" for our final deliverance.

Through Christ the King, the Holy Spirit has been poured out in preparation for his return. Let us confidently participate in this era of grace through our liturgical worship, personal prayer, and in the sacraments, those special signs that testify to the reality of Christ's kingdom already present, but not yet here in its fullness. In these ways, our actions and our lives will always speak louder than placards: "The kingdom of God, the triumph of God's plan, the end of history, *is here!*"

"Lord, as we worship you in Spirit and truth, transform us into your children and prepare us for that day when we will see you as you are, face to face."

Luke 21:34-38

34 "But take heed to yourselves lest your hearts be weighed
down with dissipation and drunkenness and cares of this life,
and that day come upon you suddenly like a snare; 35 for it will
come upon all who dwell upon the face of the whole earth.
36 But watch at all times, praying that you may have strength to
escape all these things that will take place, and to stand before
the Son of man."
37 And every day he was teaching in the temple, but at night
he went out and lodged on the mount called Olivet. 38 And
early in the morning all the people came to him in the temple
to hear him.

Sometimes it takes a major life event, like a grave illness, to show us what is really important in life. Often, we are weighed down by cares that, if we take an eternal perspective, really don't matter that much. What a blessing it would be to view things with eternity in mind every day!

Jesus warned his followers not to let their hearts be "weighed down" by the cares of this world (Luke 21:34). Instead, he said: "Watch at all times, praying that you may have strength to escape all these things that will take place, and to stand before the Son of man" (21:36). When we take Jesus' words to heart, we can begin to discern what is important in life from what is not. Suddenly, the concerns that have been burdening us and causing us anxiety are seen with spiritual eyes, and much of the pressure is relieved. Not only do the problems seem to diminish in size, we also become more confident in the Lord's power to help us.

How can we experience this grace? By standing each day before the Son of Man, we can prepare ourselves for that final day when he returns in glory. When we bare our souls to Jesus in repentance and unburden ourselves of the cares that weigh us down, he will refresh us and cleanse us. Standing before him in prayer, we can see our failings in his divine light. Then, we can repent of our sins, grow in wisdom and purity, and gain the strength to stand before him on the day of judgment.

Periodically, perhaps at the end of each month, we should take stock of ourselves and our spiritual lives by spending a little extra time with the Lord. Have we grown closer to the Lord? Where have we experienced his healing touch? Where have we been weak? Perhaps we can end each month by receiving the sacrament of Reconciliation. If we "stand before the Son of Man" in this way, we will receive his mercy and love, along with the strength to live in deeper humility and trust in him.

"Jesus, we want to be watchful. Give us the courage to humbly stand before you each day so that we will be ready to welcome you when you return in glory."

The Cross of Christ

Luke
22–23

Luke 22:1-71

1 Now the feast of Unleavened Bread drew near, which is
called the Passover. 2 And the chief priests and the scribes were
seeking how to put him to death; for they feared the people.
3 Then Satan entered into Judas called Iscariot, who was of
the number of the twelve; 4 he went away and conferred with
the chief priests and captains how he might betray him to them.
5 And they were glad, and engaged to give him money.
6 So he agreed, and sought an opportunity to betray him to them
in the absence of the multitude.
7 Then came the day of Unleavened Bread, on which the
passover lamb had to be sacrificed. 8 So Jesus sent Peter and
John, saying, "Go and prepare the passover for us, that we may
eat it." 9 They said to him, "Where will you have us prepare it?"
10 He said to them, "Behold, when you have entered the city, a
man carrying a jar of water will meet you; follow him into the
house which he enters, 11 and tell the householder, 'The Teacher
says to you, Where is the guest room, where I am to eat the
passover with my disciples?' 12 And he will show you a large
upper room furnished; there make ready." 13 And they went, and
found it as he had told them; and they prepared the passover.
14 And when the hour came, he sat at table, and the apostles
with him. 15 And he said to them, "I have earnestly desired to
eat this passover with you before I suffer; 16 for I tell you I shall
not eat it until it is fulfilled in the kingdom of God." 17 And he
took a cup, and when he had given thanks he said, "Take this,
and divide it among yourselves; 18 for I tell you that from now
on I shall not drink of the fruit of the vine until the kingdom of
God comes." 19 And he took bread, and when he had given
thanks he broke it and gave it to them, saying, "This is my body
which is given for you. Do this in remembrance of me." 20 And
likewise the cup after supper, saying, "This cup which is poured
out for you is the new covenant in my blood. 21 But behold the

hand of him who betrays me is with me on the table. [22] For the
Son of man goes as it has been determined; but woe to that man
by whom he is betrayed!" [23] And they began to question one
another, which of them it was that would do this.
[24] A dispute also arose among them, which of them was to be
regarded as the greatest. [25] And he said to them, "The kings of
the Gentiles exercise lordship over them; and those in authority
over them are called benefactors. [26] But not so with you; rather
let the greatest among you become as the youngest, and the
leader as one who serves. [27] For which is the greater, one who
sits at table, or one who serves? Is it not the one who sits at
table? But I am among you as one who serves.
[28] "You are those who have continued with me in my trials;
[29] as my Father appointed a kingdom for me, so do I appoint for
you [30] that you may eat and drink at my table in my kingdom,
and sit on thrones judging the twelve tribes of Israel.
[31] "Simon, Simon, behold, Satan demanded to have you, that
he might sift you like wheat, [32] but I have prayed for you that
your faith may not fail; and when you have turned again,
strengthen your brethren." [33] And he said to him, "Lord, I am
ready to go with you to prison and to death." [34] He said, "I tell
you, Peter, the cock will not crow this day, until you three times
deny that you know me."
[35] And he said to them, "When I sent you out with no purse or
bag or sandals, did you lack anything?" They said, "Nothing."
[36] He said to them, "But now, let him who has a purse take it,
and likewise a bag. And let him who has no sword sell his man-
tle and buy one. [37] For I tell you that this scripture must be fulfilled in me, 'And he was reckoned with transgressors'; for what
is written about me has its fulfillment." [38] And they said, "Look,
Lord, here are two swords." And he said to them, "It is enough."
[39] And he came out, and went, as was his custom, to the
Mount of Olives; and the disciples followed him. [40] And when
he came to the place he said to them, "Pray that you may not

enter into temptation." [41] And he withdrew from them about a
stone's throw, and knelt down and prayed, [42] "Father, if thou art
willing, remove this cup from me; nevertheless not my will, but
thine, be done." [43] And there appeared to him an angel from
heaven, strengthening him. [44] And being in an agony he prayed
more earnestly; and his sweat became like great drops of blood
falling down upon the ground. [45] And when he rose from prayer,
he came to the disciples and found them sleeping for sorrow,
[46] and he said to them, "Why do you sleep? Rise and pray that
you may not enter into temptation."
[47] While he was still speaking, there came a crowd, and the
man called Judas, one of the twelve, was leading them. He drew
near to Jesus to kiss him; [48] but Jesus said to him, "Judas, would
you betray the Son of man with a kiss?" [49] And when those who
were about him saw what would follow, they said, "Lord, shall we
strike with the sword?" [50] And one of them struck the slave of
the high priest and cut off his right ear. [51] But Jesus said, "No
more of this!" And he touched his ear and healed him. [52] Then
Jesus said to the chief priests and captains of the temple and
elders, who had come out against him, "Have you come out as
against a robber, with swords and clubs? [53] When I was with you
day after day in the temple, you did not lay hands on me. But
this is your hour, and the power of darkness."
[54] Then they seized him and led him away, bringing him into
the high priest's house. Peter followed at a distance; [55] and when
they had kindled a fire in the middle of the courtyard and sat
down together, Peter sat among them. [56] Then a maid, seeing
him as he sat in the light and gazing at him, said, "This man also
was with him." [57] But he denied it, saying, "Woman, I do not
know him." [58] And a little later some one else saw him and said,
"You also are one of them." But Peter said, "Man, I am not."
[59] And after an interval of about an hour still another insisted,
saying, "Certainly this man also was with him; for he is a
Galilean." [60] But Peter said, "Man, I do not know what you are

saying." And immediately, while he was still speaking, the cock
crowed. 61 And the Lord turned and looked at Peter. And Peter
remembered the word of the Lord, how he had said to him,
"Before the cock crows today, you will deny me three times."
62 And he went out and wept bitterly.
63 Now the men who were holding Jesus mocked him and beat
him; 64 they also blindfolded him and asked him, "Prophesy!
Who is it that struck you?" 65 And they spoke many other words
against him, reviling him.
66 When day came, the assembly of the elders of the people
gathered together, both chief priests and scribes; and they led
him away to their council, and they said, 67 "If you are the
Christ, tell us." But he said to them, "If I tell you, you will not
believe; 68 and if I ask you, you will not answer. 69 But from now
on the Son of man shall be seated at the right hand of the power
of God." 70 And they all said, "Are you the Son of God, then?"
And he said to them, "You say that I am." 71 And they said,
"What further testimony do we need? We have heard it ourselves
from his own lips."

Luke 23:1-56

1 Then the whole company of them arose, and brought him
before Pilate. 2 And they began to accuse him, saying, "We
found this man perverting our nation, and forbidding us to give
tribute to Caesar, and saying that he himself is Christ a king."
3 And Pilate asked him, "Are you the King of the Jews?" And he
answered him, "You have said so." 4 And Pilate said to the chief
priests and the multitudes, "I find no crime in this man." 5 But
they were urgent, saying, "He stirs up the people, teaching
throughout all Judea, from Galilee even to this place."
6 When Pilate heard this, he asked whether the man was a
Galilean. 7 And when he learned that he belonged to Herod's
jurisdiction, he sent him over to Herod, who was himself in
Jerusalem at that time. 8 When Herod saw Jesus, he was very
glad, for he had long desired to see him, because he had heard
about him, and he was hoping to see some sign done by him.
9 So he questioned him at some length; but he made no answer.
10 The chief priests and the scribes stood by, vehemently accusing
him. 11 And Herod with his soldiers treated him with contempt
and mocked him; then, arraying him in gorgeous apparel, he sent
him back to Pilate. 12 And Herod and Pilate became friends
with each other that very day, for before this they had been at
enmity with each other.
13 Pilate then called together the chief priests and the rulers
and the people, 14 and said to them, "You brought me this man
as one who was perverting the people; and after examining him
before you, behold, I did not find this man guilty of any of your
charges against him; 15 neither did Herod, for he sent him back
to us. Behold, nothing deserving death has been done by him;
16 I will therefore chastise him and release him."
18 But they all cried out together, "Away with this man, and
release to us Barabbas"— 19 a man who had been thrown into
prison for an insurrection started in the city, and for murder.

[20] Pilate addressed them once more, desiring to release Jesus;
[21] but they shouted out, "Crucify, crucify him!" [22] A third time
he said to them, "Why, what evil has he done? I have found in
him no crime deserving death; I will therefore chastise him and
release him." [23] But they were urgent, demanding with loud cries
that he should be crucified. And their voices prevailed. [24] So
Pilate gave sentence that their demand should be granted. [25] He
released the man who had been thrown into prison for
insurrection and murder, whom they asked for; but Jesus he
delivered up to their will.
[26] And as they led him away, they seized one Simon of Cyrene,
who was coming in from the country, and laid on him the cross,
to carry it behind Jesus. [27] And there followed him a great
multitude of the people, and of women who bewailed and
lamented him. [28] But Jesus turning to them said, "Daughters of
Jerusalem, do not weep for me, but weep for yourselves and for
your children. [29] For behold, the days are coming when they will
say, 'Blessed are the barren, and the wombs that never bore, and
the breasts that never gave suck!' [30] Then they will begin to say
to the mountains, 'Fall on us'; and to the hills, 'Cover us.' [31] For
if they do this when the wood is green, what will happen when it
is dry?"
[32] Two others also, who were criminals, were led away to be put
to death with him. [33] And when they came to the place which is
called The Skull, there they crucified him, and the criminals,
one on the right and one on the left. [34] And Jesus said, "Father,
forgive them; for they know not what they do." And they cast
lots to divide his garments. [35] And the people stood by,
watching; but the rulers scoffed at him, saying, "He saved others;
let him save himself, if he is the Christ of God, his Chosen
One!" [36] The soldiers also mocked him, coming up and offering
him vinegar, [37] and saying, "If you are the King of the Jews, save
yourself!" [38] There was also an inscription over him, "This is the
King of the Jews."

39 One of the criminals who were hanged railed at him, saying,
"Are you not the Christ? Save yourself and us!" 40 But the other
rebuked him, saying, "Do you not fear God, since you are under
the same sentence of condemnation? 41 And we indeed justly;
for we are receiving the due reward of our deeds; but this man
has done nothing wrong." 42 And he said, "Jesus, remember me
when you come in your kingly power." 43 And he said to him,
"Truly, I say to you, today you will be with me in Paradise."
44 It was now about the sixth hour, and there was darkness over
the whole land until the ninth hour, 45 while the sun's light
failed; and the curtain of the temple was torn in two. 46 Then
Jesus, crying with a loud voice, said, "Father, into thy hands I
commit my spirit!" And having said this he breathed his last.
47 Now when the centurion saw what had taken place, he praised
God, and said, "Certainly this man was innocent!" 48 And all
the multitudes who assembled to see the sight, when they saw
what had taken place, returned home beating their breasts.
49 And all his acquaintances and the women who had followed
him from Galilee stood at a distance and saw these things.
50 Now there was a man named Joseph from the Jewish town of
Arimathea. He was a member of the council, a good and
righteous man, 51 who had not consented to their purpose and
deed, and he was looking for the kingdom of God. 52 This man
went to Pilate and asked for the body of Jesus. 53 Then he took
it down and wrapped it in a linen shroud, and laid him in a rock-
hewn tomb, where no one had ever yet been laid. 54 It was the
day of Preparation, and the sabbath was beginning. 55 The
women who had come with him from Galilee followed, and saw
the tomb, and how his body was laid; 56 then they returned, and
prepared spices and ointments. On the sabbath they rested
according to the commandment.

A Bridge to Salvation

Luke's Passion Narrative

By Gregory Roa

When you look at Luke's telling of the passion and death of Jesus, you can't help but be struck by the sense of imminent victory that runs throughout the story. Though his last hour is upon him, Jesus continues to heal, prophesy, teach his disciples, and lead sinners to repentance. At what seems like every opportunity, Luke weaves scenes of humiliation and crucifixion with powerful signs of Jesus' glorification. It's as if Jesus' suffering and death are the catalysts that ignite a chain reaction that bursts forth into the glory of his resurrection.

All throughout Luke's Gospel, the sufferings of Jesus are inextricably linked with his glorification. At his transfiguration, for example, when Jesus appears in glory with Moses and Elijah, Luke tells us that he spoke to them, not about his resurrection or about his miracles, but about his "departure" (Luke 9:31). In a sense, Jesus' entire life was a journey in which he "set his face to go to Jerusalem" where he would be "received" (9:51) into glory by being raised up on a cross. Several times he insisted that the Messiah "must suffer many things, and be rejected . . . and be killed" (9:22; see also 13:33, 17:25).

As Luke's Gospel reaches its climax in the passion, and as Jesus' suffering and his glory come closer and closer together, let us ask the Lord to show us how we are called to share in his trials as the bridge to sharing in his triumph.

A Spiritual Battle

From the very beginning of his passion narrative, Luke draws the battle lines that will usher Jesus into his hour of suffering and glory. For Luke, Jesus' passion is the ultimate confrontation between the Son of God and the forces of evil. As the festival of Unleavened Bread drew near, Luke tells us that "Satan entered into Judas" (Luke 22:3). This disciple's "opportunity to betray" Jesus (22:6) would become the devil's "opportune time" (4:13) to return and complete the temptation he began in the desert. After three years of sparring, the final battle is set in motion.

Just before entering this battle, Jesus—anticipating his triumph—shared a final meal with his disciples. Gathered at table with them, he outlined, both in word and sacrament, how they should live in the new dispensation he was about to inaugurate. Luke's account of the last supper contains some subtle, intimate details that neither Matthew nor Mark included. At the very beginning, for instance, Luke records Jesus telling his friends, "I have earnestly desired to eat this passover with you" (Luke 22:15). Then, when he celebrated the first Eucharist with them, he said, "This is my body which is given for you. Do this in remembrance of me. . . . "This cup which is poured out for you is the new covenant in my blood" (22:19-20).

Where Matthew's and Mark's gospels stated simply that the cup was given for the "many" (Matthew 26:28; Mark 14:24), Luke's subtle shift to the words "for you" encourages his readers to accept Jesus on a personal level. The added command, "Do this in remembrance of me," points the disciples beyond themselves and their immediate circumstances. They now knew how they should recall and celebrate his victory in the company of all those whom they would bring to faith in him.

Almost immediately after this personal, intimate meal, the apostles—incredibly—became mired in a dispute about who was "the greatest" (Luke 22:24). It seems as if the devil was scheming to intrude even during this occasion. But Jesus, ever in control of events, turned this near disaster into an important revelation. He used the opportunity to identify himself clearly: "Which is the greater, one who sits at table, or one who serves? But I am among you as one who serves" (22:27). Through this interplay, Luke is beckoning all of us: "Come to the table of the Lord. The Eucharist is the revelation of Jesus, the place where he ministers to his people." It is only appropriate, then, that after his resurrection, Jesus is first recognized by his disciples in the breaking of the bread (24:30-31).

Not only did Jesus identify himself, he also clarified for his apostles who they were: "You are those who have continued with me in my trials" (Luke 22:28). Their union with Jesus' sufferings was meant to bring about a new reality, in which they would "sit on thrones judging the twelve tribes of Israel" (22:30). This promise will find its fulfillment after Pentecost, when the fledgling church—the new community of faith—is established with the apostles and their successors as its leaders. At the Last Supper, a new community was established, and Jesus would now show himself to be the perfect model of everything he taught—the perfect model for all men and women of faith.

The Model of Faith

Luke is the only one to record in such vivid detail Jesus' agony in the garden: "Being in anguish he prayed more earnestly; and his sweat became like great drops of blood falling down on the ground" (Luke 22:44). Even here, in such a dark situation, we have a hint of Jesus' impending triumph. The Greek word *agonia* was most commonly used to refer to an athlete's intense, purposeful striving to take first prize in a competition. Jesus would accept his cup of suffering because his one desire was to accomplish the Father's will and thereby destroy the power of the devil.

Now, in quick succession, Luke relates how Jesus was arrested, mocked, and beaten. Though this was the "hour" of the "power of darkness" (Luke 22:53), the messianic strength of Jesus could not be overcome. When, in a display of overwrought zeal, a disciple slashed the ear of the high priest's slave, Jesus healed him (22:50-51). Then, in the courtyard, after Peter denied his master three times, Jesus "turned and looked at Peter" (22:61) with a gaze that prompted tears of repentance. Even now, when he appeared to be helpless and defeated, Jesus continued to minister powerfully to his disciples.

Jesus was also the perfect witness as he testified to the truth before the elders, the chief priests, and scribes of Israel. He did not refuse the titles "Christ" (Luke 22:67) and "Son of God" (22:70), but sealed his own fate by proclaiming, "From now on the Son of man shall be seated at the right hand of the power of God" (22:69). Even after he was sentenced to death, as he began his walk to Golgotha, Jesus remained God's faithful prophet. He was going to his death, but he stopped to tell some women who were mourning for him, "Daughters of Jerusalem, do not weep for me, but weep for yourselves and for your children" (23:28). Through unwavering faith and trust in God's plan, Jesus maintained his union with God and, therefore, his ability to speak in a way that comforted people, even as it pierced their hearts with the truths of his gospel.

The Dawning of Salvation

Jesus began his passion by uniting himself to the Father in prayer (Luke 22:41-42), and he maintained this union to his very last moment. Even as he was crucified, he prayed, "Father, forgive them; for they know not what they do" (23:34). Forgiveness, the "lifting away" of sins, has already begun, and it will continue as Jesus' salvation breaks upon the world and his disciples bring the good news to every nation under heaven.

Another dramatic sign of the dawning of salvation is evident in the conversion of the good thief (Luke 23:39-43). This scene is all the more poignant because it happens at what seems to be the lowest point of Jesus' journey—as he hung dying on a cross, rejected by the people he loved, derided by the religious leaders, and scorned by a common criminal. Still, this raging tempest of abuse and horror is blocked out for a moment by the quiet of the repentant man's prayer, "Jesus, remember me when you come into your kingly power" (23:42). The Lord's peaceful response was in some respects a mockery of those mocking him. Despite all the insults being hurled at him—despite the piercing agony of the nails and the thorns—Jesus found the strength to respond with calm assurance: "Truly, I say to you, today you will be with me in Paradise" (23:43).

Exhausting one last gasp of wrath, all the forces of evil now sought to envelop the Crucified One, emitting a "darkness over the whole land" (Luke 23:44). Ironically, by destroying the Son of God, Satan unwittingly allowed the barrier between God and his people to be removed, symbolically indicated when the "curtain of the temple was torn in two" (23:45). It was the moment of triumph, for Jesus went to his death crying out in absolute trust: "Father, into thy hands I commit my spirit!" (23:46).

Luke ends his passion by telling us about several "witnesses" around the cross—proof that the world had already begun to change even before the resurrection. A Roman centurion, seeing Jesus' death, "praised God" and declared, "Certainly this man was innocent" (Luke 23:47). Similarly, the people who had earlier been so hostile began "beating their breasts" in repentance (23:48)—the first step toward conversion. Luke is the only writer to mention that Jesus' "acquaintances" stood by with "the women who had followed him from Galilee" (23:49). These "acquaintances," whether they were the apostles or other followers, would now give testimony to the power of Jesus' death. The final witness was Joseph of Arimathea, "a good and righteous man" (23:50) whose courage in asking for Jesus' body foreshadowed the boldness of the apostles who will testify to the risen Lord on Pentecost Sunday.

Marking the Start of Our Journey

The *Catechism of the Catholic Church* teaches that "The Paschal mystery of Christ's cross and Resurrection stands at the center of the Good News" (571). Jesus' passion was the critical phase not only for his own journey but for all of salvation history—and so for our own history as well. Jesus' final prayer on the cross unleashed the Spirit and brought forth the age of the church, whose dramatic beginnings Luke describes in his subsequent volume, the Acts of the Apostles. Flowing from the cross of Christ is the power of the Spirit, the life of the church which we continue to build until Jesus returns again.

As we look forward to the second coming, God calls all of us to live as Jesus lived: faithful to the Father's will, trusting that God will see us through our trials, loving our brothers and sisters despite their failings, showing compassion to the needy, and testifying to the reality of the kingdom of God. Like the apostles, we too are sustained in our struggle against evil by Jesus' intercession (Luke 22:32) and by partaking of his body and blood (22:19-20). And, like Simon of Cyrene (23:26), we too must be prepared at all times to take up the cross and follow the Lord on his journey to the Father. Only as we continue to die with Jesus will we know the absolute victory and triumph of his cross.

A Devotional Commentary on Luke

The Resurrection

Luke
24

Luke 24:1-12

1 But on the first day of the week, at early dawn, they went to
the tomb, taking the spices which they had prepared. 2 And
they found the stone rolled away from the tomb, 3 but when
they went in they did not find the body. 4 While they were
perplexed about this, behold, two men stood by them in dazzling
apparel; 5 and as they were frightened and bowed their faces to
the ground, the men said to them, "Why do you seek the living
among the dead? He is not here, but has risen." 6 "Remember
how he told you, while he was still in Galilee, 7 that the Son of
man must be delivered into the hands of sinful men, and be
crucified, and on the third day rise." 8 And they remembered his
words, 8 and returning from the tomb they told all this to the
eleven 9 and to all the rest. 10 Now it was Mary Magdalene and
Jo-anna and Mary the mother of James and the other women
with them who told this to the apostles; 11 but these words
seemed to them an idle tale, and they did not believe them.
12 But Peter rose and ran to the tomb; stooping and looking in,
he saw the linen cloths by themselves; and he went home
wondering at what had happened.

From a vision of Hildegard of Bingen, a 12th century Benedictine abbess and visionary:

Behold! The atmosphere suddenly rose up in a dark sphere of great magnitude, and that flame hovered over it and gave it one blow after another, which struck sparks from it, until that atmosphere was perfected and so heaven and earth stood fully formed and resplendent. Then the same flame was in that fire, and that burning extended itself to a little clod of mud which lay at the bottom of the atmosphere, and warmed it so that it was made flesh and blood, and blew upon it until it rose up a living human.

When this was done, the blazing fire, by means of that flame which burned ardently with a gentle breath, offered to the human a white flower, which hung in that flame as dew hangs on the grass. Its scent came to the human's nostrils, but he did not taste it with his mouth or touch it with his hands, and thus he turned away and fell into the thickest darkness, out of which he could not pull himself. And that darkness grew and expanded more and more in the atmosphere.

And I saw a serene Man coming forth from this radiant dawn, who poured out his brightness into the darkness; and it drove him back with great force, so that he poured out the redness of blood and whiteness of pallor into it, and struck the darkness such a strong blow that the person who was lying in it was touched by him, took on a shining appearance and walked out of it upright. And so the serene Man who had come out of the dawn shone more brightly than human tongue can tell, and made his way into the greatest height of inestimable glory, where he radiated in the plenitude of wonderful fruitfulness and fragrance.

As you see, the serene Man who has come out of that dawn shines more brightly than human tongue can tell, which shows that the noble body of the Son of God, born of the sweet Virgin and three days in the tomb (to confirm that there are three Persons in one Divinity), was touched by the glory of the Father, received the Spirit and rose again to serene immortality, which no one can explain by thought or word. And the Father showed him with his open wounds to the celestial choirs, saying, "This is my beloved Son, whom I sent to die for the people."

And so joy unmeasurable by the human mind arose in them, for criminal forgetfulness of God was brought low, and human reason, which had lain prostrate under the Devil's persuasion, was uplifted to the knowledge of God; for the way to truth was shown to man by the Supreme Beatitude, and in it he was led from death to life.

Luke 24:13-35

[13] That very day two of them were going to a village named
Emmaus, about seven miles from Jerusalem, [14] and talking with
each other about all these things that had happened. [15] While
they were talking and discussing together, Jesus himself drew
near and went with them. [16] But their eyes were kept from
recognizing him. [17] And he said to them, "What is this
conversation which you are holding with each other as you
walk?" And they stood still, looking sad. [18] Then one of them,
named Cleopas, answered him, "Are you the only visitor to
Jerusalem who does not know the things that have happened
there in these days?" [19] And he said to them, "What things?"
And they said to him, "Concerning Jesus of Nazareth, who was a
prophet mighty in deed and word before God and all the people,
[20] and how our chief priests and rulers delivered him up to be
condemned to death, and crucified him. [21] But we had hoped
that he was the one to redeem Israel. Yes, and besides all this, it
is now the third day since this happened. [22] Moreover, some
women of our company amazed us. They were at the tomb early
in the morning [23] and did not find his body; and they came back
saying that they had even seen a vision of angels, who said that
he was alive. [24] Some of those who were with us went to the
tomb, and found it just as the women had said; but him they did
not see." [25] And he said to them, "O foolish men, and slow of
heart to believe all that the prophets have spoken! [26] Was it not
necessary that the Christ should suffer these things and enter
into his glory?" [27] And beginning with Moses and all the
prophets, he interpreted to them in all the scriptures the things
concerning himself.
[28] So they drew near to the village to which they were going.
He appeared to be going further, [29] but they constrained him,
saying, "Stay with us, for it is toward evening and the day is now
far spent." So he went in to stay with them. [30] When he was at

table with them, he took the bread and blessed, and broke it,
and gave it to them. 31 And their eyes were opened and they
recognized him; and he vanished out of their sight. 32 They said
to each other, "Did not our hearts burn within us while he
talked to us on the road, while he opened to us the scriptures?" 33
And they rose that same hour and returned to Jerusalem; and
they found the eleven gathered together and those who were
with them, 34 who said, "The Lord has risen indeed, and has
appeared to Simon!" 35 Then they told what had happened on
the road, and how he was known to them in the breaking of
the bread.

How could God have abandoned Jesus, "a prophet mighty in deed and word" (Luke 24:19), to a gruesome death on the cross? This must have been the perplexing question that Cleopas and the other disciple kept posing as they spoke with their mysterious new friend on the road to Emmaus. Like all the other disciples, these two men simply could not accept on its own the account of the women who visited the empty tomb (24:22-24). Their faith was so shattered that they were "slow of heart to believe" that even Jesus could rise from the dead (24:25). As with everyone who comes to faith, they needed a work of the Spirit to reveal the Paschal truth and to allow it to take root within them. They could not come to this faith by their own will or effort or intellect alone.

As the stranger explained the scriptures to them, their hearts began to burn with faith, and they were moved to open their hearts once more (Luke 24:32). Through the word of God, the Spirit moved them to accept the good news of the resurrection, and so they pressed their friend to stay with them (24:28-29). Significantly, the point of ultimate recognition came when "their eyes were opened" as Jesus blessed and broke the bread (24:30-31).

Luke's original readers would have readily grasped the association: The disciples recognized Christ in the scriptures and knew his presence most fully through the Eucharist.

It was precisely the bodily resurrection of Christ—seen by witnesses and revealed in their hearts—which erased the scandal of the crucifixion for the early church. As Peter's first sermon affirmed: "God raised [Jesus] up, having loosed the pangs of death, because it was not possible for him to be held by it" (Acts 2:24). Jesus' resurrection gave meaning to the cross, for it showed that he was no mere man, but was God's sacrificial lamb "without blemish or spot . . . destined before the foundation of the world" (1 Peter 1:19-20).

We can cling to these great truths as our anchor in an age filled with doubt. Our confidence rests secure, because our "faith and hope are in God" who intervened in human history (1 Peter 1:21). Let us be quick to embrace the risen Savior, seeking him in word and sacrament, and inviting him to remain with us, just as the two disciples did so long ago on the way to Emmaus. As we do, the truth of Jesus risen and alive will burn in our hearts.

Luke 24:36-48

36 As they were saying this, Jesus himself stood among them,
and said to them, "Peace to you." 37 But they were startled and
frightened, and supposed that they saw a spirit. 38 And he said to
them, "Why are you troubled, and why do questionings rise in
your hearts? 39 See my hands and my feet, that it is I myself;
handle me, and see; for a spirit has not flesh and bones as you
see that I have." 40 And when he had said this, he showed them
his hands and his feet. 41 And while they still disbelieved for joy,
and wondered, he said to them, "Have you anything here to
eat?" 42 They gave him a piece of broiled fish, 43 and he took it
and ate before them.
44 Then he said to them, "These are my words which I spoke to

you, while I was still with you, that everything written about me
in the law of Moses and the prophets and the psalms must be
fulfilled." 45 Then he opened their minds to understand the
scriptures, 46 and said to them, "Thus it is written, that the
Christ should suffer and on the third day rise from the dead,
47 and that repentance and forgiveness of sins should be preached
in his name to all nations, beginning from Jerusalem.
48 You are witnesses of these things."

What an astounding turn of events! The man whom the disciples had followed for three years and with whom they traveled all over Palestine—the one they saw die on a cross—stood before them and told them that God had raised him from death. It's no wonder their lives were turned upside down. Could you be the same if this happened to you?

To assure them that his death was no accident, Jesus opened the disciples' minds to understand how everything written in the Hebrew scriptures pointed to him and was fulfilled in him. From first to last, Jesus Christ is the fulfillment of everything God has spoken to his creation. Throughout history, God was working meticulously, preparing for the moment when his Son would come to earth to win our forgiveness. Each event spoken of in scripture, each prophetic promise, each prayer and wise saying, is part of an intricate mosaic that reveals another aspect of our triune God and his love for his people. From the very start, God has been speaking to us about his Son, drawing us in so many ways to embrace the life that Jesus came to give us.

Even today, 2,000 years after the resurrection, Jesus remains the summation of God's words to us. The gospels are filled with stories of encounters with the risen Lord to show us that we too can know Jesus Christ, risen from the dead. Jesus did not simply ascend to heaven, there to remain hidden until the second coming. He rose in glory, and he wants to share the hope and joy of his resurrection with all his people. He wants us all to receive his divine life, to know a life that is victorious over sin and death.

Just as Jesus opened the disciples' minds to see him in scripture, he wants to do the same for us. We can experience his love and presence as we ponder his words with a quiet heart. God wants to show us that it has always been his desire and plan to give up his only Son so that we could be reconciled to God and share in his divine life.

"Heavenly Father, send your Spirit to reveal your Son Jesus to us. Fill our hearts with gratitude for the new life you offer. Open our eyes to see your wonderful plan for us—a plan which you have revealed in your word of scripture."

Luke 24:49-53

49 And behold, I send the promise of my Father upon you; but
stay in the city, until you are clothed with power from on high."
50 Then he led them out as far as Bethany, and lifting up his
hands he blessed them. 51 While he blessed them, he parted
from them, and was carried up into heaven. 52 And they
worshipped him, and returned to Jerusalem with great joy,
53 and were continually in the temple blessing God.

How quickly those days with Jesus after he rose from the dead must have passed for the disciples. How amazed must they have been when he told them he would be leaving them once more. Now, having ascended, Jesus could fulfill all his promises to his followers.

Reunited with the Father, Jesus could now be present with the disciples everywhere and at all times: With Philip in Samaria, John on Patmos, and Peter in Rome. He could be present not just in their affections and their memories, but in reality and power. He could work throughout the entire earth, not merely in a neglected corner of the Roman empire. Now he could pour out the Spirit in fullness.

This is why the church celebrates Ascension Day. It does not signal Jesus' withdrawal from the building of God's kingdom. Instead, it is the decisive establishment of Jesus' lordship. Consider these words written by William Temple (1881-1944), Archbishop of Canterbury:

> The ascension of Christ is his liberation from all restrictions of time and space. It does not represent his removal from the earth, but his constant presence everywhere on earth.
>
> During his earthly ministry he could only be in one place at a time. If he was in Jerusalem he was not in Capernaum; if he was in Capernaum he was not in Jerusalem. But now he is united with God, he is present wherever God is present; and that is everywhere. Because he is in heaven, he is everywhere on earth; because he is ascended, he is here now. In the person of the Holy Spirit he dwells in his church, and issues forth from the deepest depths of the souls of his disciples, to bear witness to his sovereignty.

What an amazing plan of salvation! How completely is our God committed to building humanity into a united body, and body of Christ. What a rich grace for us to treasure as we dedicate ourselves to the work of the church!

No, Jesus did not leave us alone to struggle in quiet desperation. He departed from us in order to send the Third Person of the Trinity, to make eternal intercession for us before God's throne, and to prepare for that day when he will return to deliver the fullness of God's kingdom to those who retain the deposit of faith.

Topical Index of Luke's Gospel

Events in the Life of Jesus: